Conversations with Horses: An In-Depth Look at Signals & Cues between Horses and their Humans

by

Hertha James

Powerword Publications,

Palmerston North, New Zealand

Muddy Horse Coaching

hertha.james@xtra.co.nz

www.safehorse.info

www.herthamuddyhorse.com

This updated version 2017

Font: Bookman Old Style 11

Disclaimer of liability:

Horses that show dangerous behaviors should not be paired with casual/inexperienced horse owners/handlers.

Risk Radar: When around horses, we must have our Risk Radar on at all times.

Cover Photograph by Adam Evans

Some of the photographs are taken from video footage which decreases quality but allows illustration of an exact movement or moment.

ISBN-13 978-1514388945

ISBN-10 1514388944

Contents

Other Books

The following books are also available from Amazon.com as hard copy or as e-books.

They contain lots of background material and specific Training Plans, with free links to YouTube clips.

You can find them any time by putting my name (Hertha James) into the Amazon search engine.

- **How to Begin Equine Clicker Training**: *Improve Horse-Human Communication*
- **Walking with Horses**: *The Eight Leading Positions*
- **Learn Universal Horse Language**: *No Ropes*
- **How to Create Good Horse Training Plans**: *The Art of Thin-Slicing*

If you prefer e-books but don't have a Kindle reader, Amazon has a free Kindle reader which can be downloaded to any computer, tablet or smartphone.

This book includes:

Eight Training Plans

The Training Plans can be used as springboards for creating your own Individual Education Programs for specific horses.

Free links to illustrative short video clips via YouTube

Find my YouTube channel with a search for *Hertha Muddyhorse*. Please see the end of the book for a comprehensive list of titles. Relevant video clips are also mentioned throughout the book.

These playlists mainly relate to the ideas in this book:

1. *HorseGym with Boots*: these are numbered. For example, if you would like to view Clip #18, simply put "*#18 HorseGym with Boots*" into the YouTube search engine and it should take you there. Each title starts with its number.

2. *Starting Clicker training*: some older clips when the horses were just learning about Clicker training.

3. *Free-Shaping*: these clips only have names. To find one, click on the playlist name and scroll down to find the title that you want.

4. *Thin-Slicing*: these clips also only have names so please scroll down the list to find the title you want to view.

Short video clips naturally have their limitations, but hopefully they will help illustrate some of the concepts and provide fuel for developing your own training ideas.

The Author

The author's background:

- Zoologist (BSc Calgary)
- Zookeeper (Calgary, Canada & Wellington, NZ)
- Animal handler & continuity on movie sets (Canada)
- Teacher of high school Science and Biology for 23 years (Diploma of Teaching, Christchurch, New Zealand)
- Diploma of Information and Library Science (Wellington, NZ)
- Lifelong interest in understanding animals, especially horses, which have always been part of her life
- Years with dogs and dog obedience competition
- Keen international Horse Agility participant
- Two times gold medal winner in the World Clicker Equine Games
- Has written extensive teaching and learning resources and occasional fiction

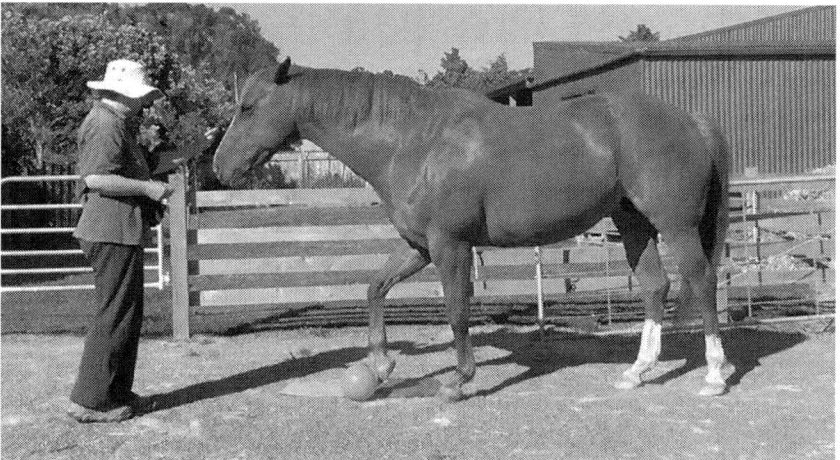

Playing with Boots bursting balloons.

Introduction

It is my hope that this book will help people enjoy the company of their horses, ponies, donkeys and mules in contexts other than riding. Working and playing on the ground with our horses can be great recreation for us and the horse.

A horse with lovely ground manners is a pleasure. Many riders, once they are aware of the many things we can do with ground work, find it such fun that riding becomes an extra bonus.

Taking a well-mannered horse, pony or donkey for a walk can be a wonderful pastime.

Figure 1: The new word for walking our horse instead of our dog is 'equicising'.

The newish sport of Horse Agility, done with the horse on a lead or at liberty can provide monthly challenges that give focus to our training. As well as providing new challenges, it highlights 'training holes' that we can remedy.

Horses enjoy the stimulation of learning new things if they are taught in a way that makes sense to them. Playing with our horses on the ground gives them the mental, emotional and physical stimulation necessary for a healthy life. It also makes them a pleasure to be with.

*Figure 2: Col and Ash practicing the S-bend
Horse Agility obstacle.*

However, to be safe, we must make sure some ground rules are in place. I walk my horse daily and she is better behaved on her lead than many people's dogs.

Of course, it wasn't always like that. As an eighteen-month-old youngster, with little handling and very strong ideas of her own, she was a major challenge to my skills at the time.

This book looks mainly at the way we can communicate with our horse on the ground. The relationship built there carries over into riding if we also want to ride.

Whether we ride or not, all domestic horses need the life skills to be confident with their human handlers for everyday management and care. Since we have taken the horse away from his natural existence, it is up to us to teach him those life skills.

Why Walk with Horses?

If we are with our horse but not on him, we are 'walking with him'. How we walk with him and handle his lead rope makes a huge difference to how he perceives us.

In no particular order, here are some reasons to walk with our horse beyond his daily care routine.

1. Horse too young to ride
2. Horse too old to ride
3. Horse can't be ridden due to past injury
4. Horse is recovering from current injury
5. Horse too small to ride (some people love ponies)
6. Not enough time to ride
7. Horse lives in enclosed space and needs to get out frequently to aid blood circulation and maintain good mental state
8. To take horse to nice grazing spots not otherwise available
9. To take horse out to get used to the wider world — building confidence
10. Person not physically able to ride
11. Person not confident enough to ride a particular horse at a particular time
12. Person wants to establish a relationship with the horse — become part of the horse's world and be accepted by the horse as at least one rank higher than the horse in the social order within which the horse is living
13. Person wants to transition barefoot horse with daily short walks on hard surfaces
14. Person wants the exercise and enjoys being out and about with their horse for company. We walk with our dogs, so why not our horses?
15. To begin (or re-do) the education of the horse in all the mini-skills it needs to live comfortably in the human environment. Here are some examples.

   - Learn to follow a feel on the halter.
   - Learn to move away from pressure (instinct is to move into it).
   - Learn disengagement of the hind end.

- Learn to shift the shoulders over.
- Loose-rope leading following human body language signals.
- Transitions — learn synchronicity with a moving person just as they would synchronize with other horses in their group (drive & draw).
- Learn backing-up on request.
- Learn moving sideways on request.
- Learn vertical flexion at the poll on request.
- Learn lateral flexion of the neck on request.
- Learn horizontal (lateral) flexion of the whole body on request.
- Learn moving out on a circle on request, without feeling that they are being 'sent away'.
- Learn to navigate obstacles, water, tight spots, trailers, wash-bays, chutes.
- Learn the feel of a saddle or harness doing all the above, before riding/driving is started.
- All the above as a basis for playing with a horse at liberty (no halter/lead).

A Few General Concepts

It is only from the person's calm, centered core that meaningful teaching can proceed. And it is only from the horse's calm, centered core that meaningful learning can take place.

When we become more mindful about what our body is doing, it is easier for the horse to read our intention and our signal.

The horse will often let us know which signal makes the most sense to him. We just need to listen.

No matter how we try to put a gloss on it, our horse is captive to a foreign species whose language is foreign.

Horses don't do things to annoy us. At any moment in time the horse is doing what he believes is the best thing to do.

The key to being with horses safely is to understand how to be assertive without being aggressive.

If a horse is using body language so strong that we fear for our safety, that horse has not had a smooth introduction to positive interactions with people.

We often like to romanticize wild horses, but there is not much romantic about a life lived in the environmental margins of the plains and mountains where wild horses survive in the 21st century.

The more we realize that much of what we are communicating to the horse is in our unconscious body language, the more we can silence our body between meaningful signals.

The more we become aware of our breathing and how it relates our energy level to the horse, the more fun it is to use our breathing as a key signal to communicate our intent.

It is not 'footfall' we need to feel as we lead or ride the horse, as much as 'foot-rise'. It is only at the moment that the foot is rising that we can influence where it goes next.

Riding is merely an extension of 'guiding from behind' on the ground. We are guiding the horse from behind his drive line (everything behind his withers).

It is the most natural thing in the world to want the horse to change so it does what we want it to do. However, it is by changing what we do that yields the results we want.

Each horse/handler partnership is unique, so only the horse's handler can write a horse's Individual Education Program.

Ideally, we want to teach in a way that keeps the horse being continually successful. We want the horse to maintain his confidence with each part of the teaching/learning process.

My Aim

My aim with this work is to raise awareness about:

1. The variety of signals we use
2. The importance of our body orientation as a signal
3. The importance of consistency with our body language and our gestures
4. How we use halter touch pressure via ropes
5. How we use rein touch pressure via bits or side-pull bridles
6. How sensitive horses are to direct touch — an invasion of their personal space
7. How grooming, foot care, massage, saddling and riding impact the horse's sense of personal space
8. How we can communicate many things with gesture only, no direct touch needed
9. How careful we should be about using verbal signals — avoiding verbal diarrhea
10. The importance of the pauses between our signals
11. The importance of how we use the marker signal (e.g., the click) when we use positive (reward) reinforcement often called clicker training
12. The importance of being aware of the environmental signals our horse is picking up
13. How we can simplify teaching/learning by setting up environmental signals for the horse, such as lanes, circles of markers, unusual surfaces, narrow spaces, nose and foot target destinations
14. The timing, intensity and duration of the signals we are using
15. Picking the right opportunity to give a signal
16. Creating ample opportunities to teach/learn a signal
17. How we can get more clarity with 'multi-signals'
18. How we can clarify our signals
19. How we can refine our signals.

This list is a bit mind-boggling but posting it in the barn means I review it often. It helps to keep at least some of the ideas in the forefront of my mind when I am out with my horse.

We'll begin by reviewing the unique biological characteristics of horses. Then we'll look at a quick overview of signal types before delving into the detail of each type of signal. The aim is to make us more mindful about what our signals are, and how we are using them.

The Natural Life of Horses

Horse sensitivity and perception of the world is much sharper than ours. Their nervous system is set up to be wary of anything different. They are genetically programmed to flee first and ask questions second. The horse natural lifestyle is also quite different from ours, with a 24/7 rhythm of eating, moving, resting.

Their digestive system requires constant small amounts of coarse fodder to keep the gut bacteria happy. The gut bacteria break down the coarse fodder and gradually release nutrients into the horse's system. When the gut bacteria are upset, horses are in trouble. When we feed our horse, it helps to consider instead, that we are feeding the gut bacteria

Horses rest between bursts of grazing over 24 hours, quite unlike the day and night rhythm of humans. Horses have strong night vision with the biggest eyes of all land animals.

The health of the horse's blood/circulatory system is closely linked to extensive movement over 24 hours. The compression and expansion of the natural foot, at each step, plays a crucial role in returning blood from the feet back to the heart, from where it is sent to the lungs to release carbon dioxide waste and gain oxygen to distribute around the body.

If we watch grazing horses, they continuously walk along, one step at a time. In the wild, food is often scarce and horses move long distances to their water sources. Freedom of movement is crucial to good horse health.

Horses are not physically designed to carry weight on their back. Their spine is delicate. Their shoulder blades 'float' on the skeleton at either side of the withers. YouTube has helpful video clips that can be found by searching for 'horse skeleton' or a similar search term.

Their skin is sensitive. Their mouths are delicate. Their finely tuned muzzle and eyebrow whiskers allow them to keep their nose and eyes safe searching for food at night or in dense vegetation. The structure of their legs and feet is highly specialized.

Each Horse is Unique

When we bring a horse into our life, we find that they come without user manuals or 'help' buttons.

A horse is not just a horse. Horses obviously come in a variety of breeds and sizes. They may come to us from the wild, from convivial horse-friendly backgrounds, from neglect, from abuse or from pharmaceutical facilities where they are exploited for human benefit in mind-numbing ways.

Each horse comes with a distinctive character type. Getting the best out of a horse that tends to be nervous and flighty requires skills different from those needed to motivate an energy-conserving, confident horse whose main goal is the next blade of grass.

Which is not to say that there won't be times when our energy-conserving (some people call them 'lazy') horse won't lose his confidence and become temporarily nervous and flighty.

Likewise, with consistent appropriate education, the nervous, flighty horse can become more confident to stay tuned in longer, rather than rush off the instant his comfort zone is breached.

The communication skills needed to get along with a bold, exuberant horse are not the same as the skills needed to bring out the confidence of an anxious horse who tends to withdraw and freeze under pressure.

More about character types is available in my book, *How to Create Good Horse Training Plans*.

Horses are endlessly fascinating. Their history in the company of humans is a checkered one full of pain and humiliation and destruction of spirit. Horses suffer quietly because they can't squeal like pigs. No doubt if they could, people would cut their vocal cords.

The advent of natural horsemanship in all its guises has brought many people a little bit closer to understanding the complexity of horses. However, we can never have enough 'help' buttons to find information and ideas about how to relate meaningfully to a particular horse and how to establish two-way communication with any horse.

The information in a book is necessarily presented in a linear way, but the Table of Contents enables you to move easily between the various sections to access the parts most relevant to you at the moment.

We'll be looking at:

1. Closing the gap between the romantic ideas many people have about horses and the reality of actually being with horses.
2. How we can get better at understanding what the horse is saying to us.
3. How we can make our signals as clear as possible so the horse can understand us most easily.
4. The different sorts of signals we can use.
5. Becoming aware of the signals we are sending unconsciously.
6. How carefully we need to design a signal and then use it with perfect consistency.
7. How we can teach the horse 90% of what he needs to know with interesting and comprehensive ground work.

1. Signals versus 'Cues' or 'Stimuli'

In the horse world, there are several terms used for the signals we give horses. One is 'aids' which is commonly used when riding. The term 'cue' seems to have become popular with clicker trainers.

Much more about Clicker Training is available in my book, *How to Begin Equine Clicker Training*. The term 'stimulus' comes from animal behavior laboratories.

I prefer the term 'signal' because it suggests that a message is sent and the 'correct' or intended message is received by the other party.

If a Morse code sender carefully sends his message, but the person at the other end does not know Morse code well enough to decode the message accurately, then the signal has failed. The garbled message may well lead to troubled times.

In other words, if a signal does not relay the desired message, then whatever we have used as a signal is not acting as a signal. By definition, a signal must communicate the person's message and be received as such by the other party, in this case, the horse.

If it is not working as intended, the signal needs to be adjusted or changed so the message sent equals the message received.

When we are with the horse, he is busy sending us signals about his emotional, mental and physical well-being. If we can't pick up these signals accurately, then the horse becomes frustrated and misunderstood and often retreats from willing interaction by trying to leave or 'shutting down'. He becomes reactive rather than responsive.

Cues and stimuli are constantly bombarding all of us. A signal is something we want to stand out from everything else the horse is noticing and everything else we are noticing. We want the horse to easily separate our signal from all the other many cues that are constantly flowing in.

At the same time, we are communicating our intent with our signals, the horse is trying hard to communicate his intent and his feelings with his body language. The more 'in tune' we can get with the signals our horse sends us, the better our two-way communication can become.

In this work, I will use the term 'signal' rather than 'aid', 'cue' or 'stimulus'. I'll also refer to all horses as 'he' for ease of reading, unless I'm talking about a specific mare or filly.

Like the rest of us, horses thrive on clarity and consistency of communication.

Building a relationship with a horse is like locating a set of keys to unlock a door so the horse's true nature can come out.

The horse's total well-being depends on how well we can help him adapt to the peculiar life a horse must live in a human-centered world.

While we are trying to get to know our horse better and understand his emotional, mental and physical boundaries, the horse is doing exactly the same with us.

He is trying to read our intentions so he can be ready to react or respond, according to his perceptions. The more we understand about the signals we are giving the horse, the more we can develop a mutual language.

The more we realize that much of what we are communicating to the horse is in our unconscious body language, the more we can 'still' our body between meaningful signals.

We would like the horse to respond confidently to our requests rather than become anxious, reactive and bracing against the pressure of our signals.

The horse would also prefer to respond rather than become anxious, adrenalized and feeling the need to react by trying to escape, push through pressure or mentally and physically 'shut down' - hiding inside himself.

A horse needs a sound foundation of knowledge to enable him to cope with the very strange things people expect of their captive horses.

To do this we need to:
- take the horse through a careful education program
- set up a teaching schedule suited to the individual horse's background and ability and adapted continually to the feedback the horse gives us
- give him every opportunity to master each small step of a large task, before asking him to string all the parts of a big task together.

This cutting of a whole task into its smallest teachable parts can be referred to as 'Thin-Slicing the task'.

My book, *How to Create Good Horse Training Plans,* looks in detail at Thin-Slicing and writing Individual Education Programs (IEPs).

For each step of the teaching process, we have to make sure we are sending a clear message rather than a confusing mumble. A key element for the success of any teaching and learning program is ensuring that our signals are consistent and clear.

Horses are so sensitive that if we alter a signal even a little bit, they often think it means something else. The more different things we teach our horse, the more carefully we need to think about the signals we use.

The more aware we can be about:
- the specific types of signals we can use
- how we are orientating our body
- how we can refine our signals as the horse becomes confident
- how we often use a 'signal bundle' or 'multi-signal'
- when we are 'nagging' rather than communicating,

the better the deal we can give the horse.

It is the most natural thing in the world to want the horse to change so it does what we want it to do. However, in reality, it is by changing what we do that yields the results we want.

There will be variations in horse behavior based on each horse's innate character type, his personal history, and the situation of the moment.

Horses will always be horses and will respond in the way that horses respond. Being prey animals, their main concern is safety.

Before we can cause change in the horse, we have to become hyper aware of what we are doing while the horse is watching.

Whenever we are in our horse's view, he is picking up all sorts of signals from us – our posture, our energy level, our intent, what we usually do that time of day, any specific signal we may be giving and so on.

Once we learn to pay close attention to the horse's body language, we get better at understanding the signals the horse is sending us.

A signal is a direct, purposeful communication between horse and handler. If we've carefully taught a signal for backing up, then the horse will back up when we give that signal.

If the horse raises his head and points his ears with strong concentration, we pick up his signal that something in the environment has his full attention.

First, we learn the horse's language – his signals. Then we have to teach the horse the language he needs to remain safe and comfortable in the human world – our signals.

Since we have taken the horse away from his natural lifestyle and made him our captive, it is up to us to become fluent in Universal Horse Language and learn to use it effectively. To be effective we need:

- an understanding of different horse character types
- an understanding of our particular horse's character type
- awareness of our body language and the different ways we use signals
- knowledge about horse senses and sensitivity

- as much knowledge as possible about a particular horse's background experiences
- adept use of body language, body extensions, ropes, reins
- timely application of release reinforcement
- to write good training plans which can be turned into individual education programs (IEPs) designed for a specific horse
- adept use of reward reinforcement along with release reinforcement.

There is detailed information about using reward reinforcement in my book, *How to Begin Equine Clicker Training.*

The more fluent we are about understanding horse body language and using the mechanics of release and reward reinforcement, the better a teacher we can be for our horse.

It is hard for the horse to learn from someone who doesn't have a good understanding of who and what they are teaching.

Before we head into an overview of the signals we use with horses, followed by a detailed look at each signal type, we need to look at how horses sense and perceive their environment.

Once we are conscious of the biological differences between horse and human perception, it is easier to allow horses the leeway they need to feel safer in our company.

2. Sensitivity of Horses

**Horses and humans don't
see & feel the world in the same way.**

2-1: Visually

Shape of the lens:

The lens of a horse eye is not able to change shape as easily as the lens of a human eye. Horse vision more resembles looking through a trifocal lens. A trifocal lens supports distance focus in one part of the lens, mid-distance focus in another part and close-up focus in a third part.

This explains why horses need to do so much positioning of their heads to see clearly. They need to raise their head high for clearer distance vision and drop it down low to get a better view of something closer.

Forcing a horse to keep his nose vertical with the ground restricts his visual field a great deal. It is easy to try this yourself.

Stand with your head up and note your field of vision. Then drop your head so your nose points to the ground. Note your field of vision now.

For a prey animal who depends on early detection of danger and a flight response for survival, restricting the field of vision by requiring (or forcing) vertical flexion can cause a lot of mental anxiety and related damaging muscle tension.

Eyes set in the side of the head:

Being set either side of a large head, horse eyes work more independently than human eyes. The positioning of the eyes limits the horse's binocular vision (being able to focus on something in front with both eyes) to a triangular area in front.

The shape of his nose causes a blind spot that extends about three feet directly in front when his head is straight, so his field of binocular vision is beyond that.

As well as his zone of binocular vision straight ahead, the horse can see almost 180 degrees beside and behind with each eye, similar to a person using rear-view mirrors on a car.

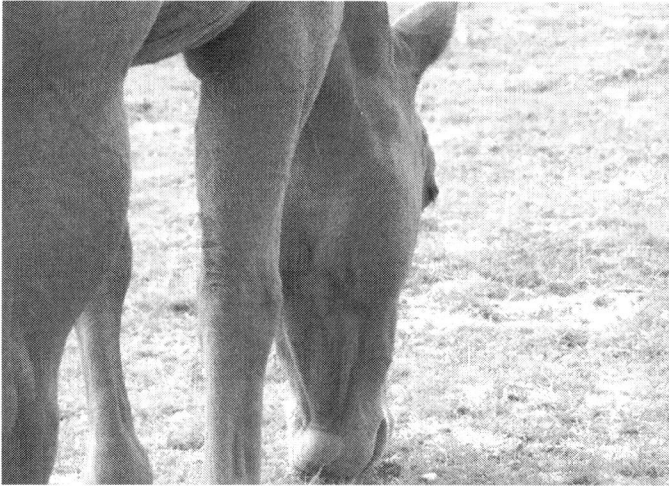

Figure 3: A horse can see almost 180 degrees on either side with his head up or down.

This side or peripheral vision is not as exact as binocular vision, but it is excellent at picking up motion. That is why horses often jump away sideways first, then turn and face the source of the motion to get a clearer picture.

When the horse is strongly focused forward using his binocular vision, his mind is busy with that and not linked to his peripheral vision. It helps explain why we need to be careful approaching a horse from the side or the back, as he can be genuinely startled by movement behind, if his attention was on something in front of him.

It also seems that horses can doze with their eyes open. So if a horse looks very relaxed, with low head, floppy bottom lip, relaxed ears and a cocked hip, he may be too asleep to notice our approach even though his eyes are open. It always pays to give a warning 'nicker' or say something in such a situation.

Light Intensity:

With their extremely large eyes, horses have excellent night vision as long as there is some environmental light. I can vouch for this, having once been caught on the far side of a hydro river, when water was unexpectedly released into the river from the dam upstream, during a sunset ride. We had to ride in serious darkness on an unknown track to reach the dam and cross over to our home side.

Horse eyes take longer than our eyes to adjust from light to dark or dark to light. It's important to remember this when we move a horse from a dark building into bright sunlight or from sunlight into a dark truck or trailer. We should allow him to stand with his head in the entrance while his vision adjusts.

Blind Spots:

Horses have a triangular blind spot that reaches about a meter in front of their nose. That is why they need to lower their head as they approach an object closely to inspect it.

You can simulate what it is like, to have a long nose like a horse, by putting your hands in place as in the photo below. Note how it affects your ability to see right in front of your nose.

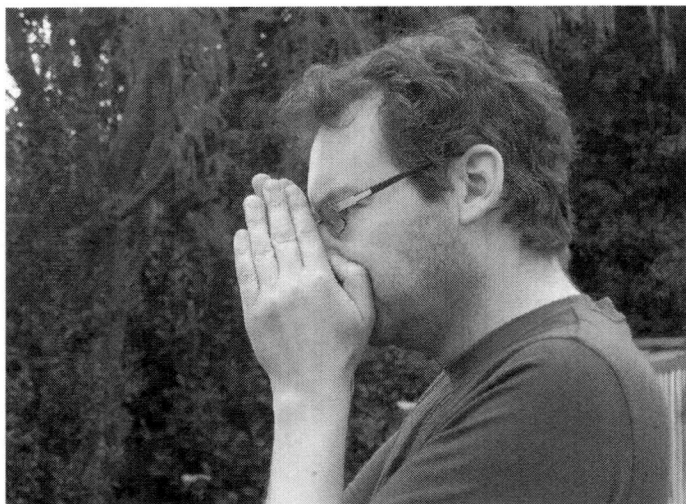

Figure 4: Alex demonstrates how to place your hands to imitate a horse's long nose to give you an idea of the nature of a horse's blind spot when they are looking straight ahead.

They also have a blind spot right behind their tail if their head is straight.

If we are experimenting to find the best position to give our horses a visual signal, it pays to be aware of how their vision differs from ours.

Depth Perception:

A horse's small range of binocular vision makes depth perception tricky, so they again need to raise and lower their head to compare the object of interest with things they have seen before. This comparison of the look of 'new things' with things already in the horse's memory, helps explain why horses are so sensitive to anything which has been changed, added or subtracted to what was there the last time they passed by.

This limited depth perception explains why horses are often reluctant to step into a puddle. The reflected light and the 'unknown' surface' under the water are both problematic. Soft mud can easily compromise a horse's ability to flee if the need arises.

The horse eye has a 'visual streak' in the retina (sensory screen at the back of the eye) which is the area of most accurate vision. Horses move their heads in order to bring the item of interest into the range of this 'visual streak' to improve the depth perception and detail of the image.

If the horse's head is restricted by tight ropes or reins, his ability to see clearly is compromised. Not surprisingly, such restrictions cause tension that affects the whole body.

Horse eyes appear to magnify objects more than our eyes (maybe up to 50%). The acuity (sharpness) of what they see is less than 20/20 human vision, but seems to be better than that of dog and cat vision.

Training in Both Eyes:

The way horse vision works helps explain why it is so important to teach everything we do on both sides of the horse. A horse that is only handled from the left side will suffer from 'right eye neglect'. Handling procedures will be 'strange' to his mind on that side because the neglect means no nerve pathways have formed to build his confidence with handling on the right side.

This links in to all aspects of training and handling. Like us, horses are naturally either left or right handed. In other words, like us, their bodies are asymmetrical.

Unless both sides of the horse's body are coached gymnastically, it is hard for the horse to be straight in his body. Which means a saddle will always be misaligned to some extent. A symmetrical saddle on an asymmetrical horse is a perennial problem for riders and painful for horses.

When teaching a new movement, the less agile side of the body needs at least two or three times more attention than the agile side of the body. Think about the trouble we have brushing our teeth with our non-dominant hand.

Environmental visual signals:

Horses living within sight of their owner's house use the lights coming on during a winter morning as a signal that their morning feed is not far away. Parts of the year I provide a hay net in the late evening. The headlamp I wear provides my horse with a visual signal and she often meets me at the stable.

During ground work our body language and gestures are visual signals. Even if we are long-reining, the horse is usually able to see us by turning his head (as long as he is not wearing blinkers).

When my horse's companion, a large white gelding, went to live elsewhere, her attention was often riveted on a white Charolaise cow in a distant paddock as she tried to figure out whether that was her old paddock mate.

My thoroughbred mare, Gypsy, was super conscious of anything on the distant horizon. A rabbit hunter toting a rifle, so far away that I could barely see him, caught her immediate attention.

Awareness Needed:

Horses are genetically wired to pay close attention to anything different:
- to how it looked before or
- that wasn't there before.

Because their eyes are not the same as ours, it is important to be aware of the following situations.

- Depending on the shape of the horse's belly, there is also a blind spot under his hind legs and under his belly. If we ask a horse to back over a rail, he can't actually see the rail at the time, but is working from memory or feel. Just because we can see it doesn't mean the horse can see it!
- When we approach the horse from the front, it is best to be just off center so we are not in his front blind spot.
- If the horse is focused on something ahead in his area of binocular vision, his mind is not engaged with his peripheral vision. This means that something suddenly moving toward him from behind can result in a startle response, often called 'spooking'. Peripheral vision picks up movement rather than detail, so the horse will want to turn and inspect the cause of the spook, either by wheeling around or running first; then turning when he feels safe enough to have a look.
- If we are doing ground work behind the horse, we need to move between his right and left peripheral vision and teach him to adjust his head so he learns to confidently keep us in view as we move left and right into and out of his blind spot.

- When horses negotiate a jump, the jump disappears from their vision as they approach it, so they are jumping from their memory of where the jump is. If the horse was paying attention to something else on the approach to the jump, he will run right into it without realizing it is there.

When we move from ground work to riding, the visual signals the horse has learned suddenly disappear. If we teach the relevant 'touch' and verbal signals during our ground work, we make it easier for the horse to navigate the change to riding. Once mounted we need to carefully teach the replacement 'touch' signals by at first pairing them with the verbal and visual signals the horse already understands from his ground work.

If touch and verbal signals are clearly taught with ground work, the switch to riding can simply be part of a systematic progression rather than a major change.

2-2: Hearing

It's hard for us to understand how much better horses hear than we do. Sounds or words easily become signals if we use them consistently. Sounds can also be environmental signals the horse adopts according to the routines of his captivity.
- door opening if the horse lives near the handler's house
- person's car arriving at the paddock (with special feed, treats or anticipated adventures)
- rattle of food buckets or pellets in a tin
- whistle to come in for a treat or a feed

We fine tune this response to sound when we use a click or unique sound to mark the precise response we want when we use Clicker Training.

Horse ears have ten muscles each, enabling the ears to move almost 180 degrees. The shape of the ear allows the horse to capture more sound, and from further away, than our ears.

On top of that, horses can pick up sounds in a higher and lower frequency range than we can.

The shape and mobility of the two ears allows accurate gauging of the direction of a sound. Sound and vision are obviously closely linked. Due to the horse's ecosystem role as a prey animal, he is wired to notice any unusual sound, especially sneaky or unusual sounds.

Horses have strong emotional responses to sounds. Anxious type horses will find the sounds and tense atmosphere of shows and events over-stimulating and problematic. It helps to gradually habituate them to this sort of environment rather than depend on flooding (overstimulation until the horse 'shuts down') to get a horse more able to cope with noisy, unfamiliar surroundings.

It seems that horses also pick up vibrations from the ground through their feet or through their whiskers and teeth while grazing. No doubt this relates to the 'early warning' horses and other animals can give us about earthquakes and other catastrophes. It might also be why they are waiting at the gate before they can see our car. But that could also be a function of their hearing.

2-3: Senses of Smell and Taste

Horses need strong senses of smell and taste. Safe grazing requires horses to be constantly aware of poisonous plants. Horses are adept at picking the best forage out of a pasture. Unless they are starving, they stay well clear of plants like buttercup and ragwort.

By sniffing a horse dropping, a horse can identify its owner. In the wild, horse droppings mark home range boundaries and leave a clear message to other horses about who lives here.

When we bring out a tube of worming paste, our horse knows what it is. Vets have a distinctive smell. Since every horse, dog and person has a distinctive smell, horses recognize us or old friends after long absences.

They similarly recognize individuals they don't like. In the wild, horses identify each predator by its distinctive smell.

If we toss a treat onto the ground, the horse has to sniff it out because it will be in his visual blind spot. On our morning walks, my mare often busies herself sniffing things on the road surface.

To ensure grazing safety, taste is well developed. To some extent, horses can 'spit out' something they don't like, but not as well as dogs or people. They are not able to vomit.

Sometimes horses are reluctant to drink water that tastes different to the water at home so people teach them to drink water with a bit of apple cider vinegar or molasses added (before they leave home).

They are also very astute about knowing when their regular feed has been doctored with medications. I have to hide medicine in jam sandwiches for Boots.

Horses can develop a lively set of 'acquired tastes'. My mare loves tomatoes, celery, parsley, peaches (she elegantly spits out the stones), feijoa, mandarins, bananas and plucks the odd lemon off the tree as she walks past.

She is less keen on cucumber, lettuce or spinach. My friend's horse, Smoky, did not have such a refined palate and would distastefully drop anything unusual out of his mouth.

2-4: Touch

Whisker Touch

Whiskers are an important 'early warning system' to protect a horse's eyes, nose and muzzle. Grazing in the dark or in tall grass requires sensitivity that functions with touch.

Each whisker has its own nerve pathway connecting directly to the brain. There may only be two long and several short whiskers around each eye, but they are enough to keep the eye safe in most circumstances.

It is therefore sad to see 'show horses' with whiskers cut or shaved off. Because people don't have comparable 'touch sensitivity' organs they incorrectly presume that a horse does not need his whiskers.

My horse uses her muzzle whiskers to check if an electric fence is on or off.

Nose Touch

When a horse investigates something new, his first act is often to carefully put his whiskers on it, then his whole nose. The mobile part of the horse's nose and upper lip have touch sensitivity similar to that of human fingers.

Foot Touch

Horses know that if their feet are compromised, they are an easy meal for the first predator that comes along. Unshod feet, working in the way evolution intended, feel the nature of the ground, helping the horse adjust his balance moment to moment.

A horse asked to step onto an unusual surface will often sniff it first, then paw with a foot to gain more information about the nature of the surface. When we introduce a new surface, it is helpful for the horse if we let him paw away until his curiosity is fully satisfied.

When I introduced my horse, Boots, to a tarp for the first time, she pawed it into a scrunched-up ball. She did this the first five times I brought out the tarp. After that, she was comfortable walking over it or standing on it.

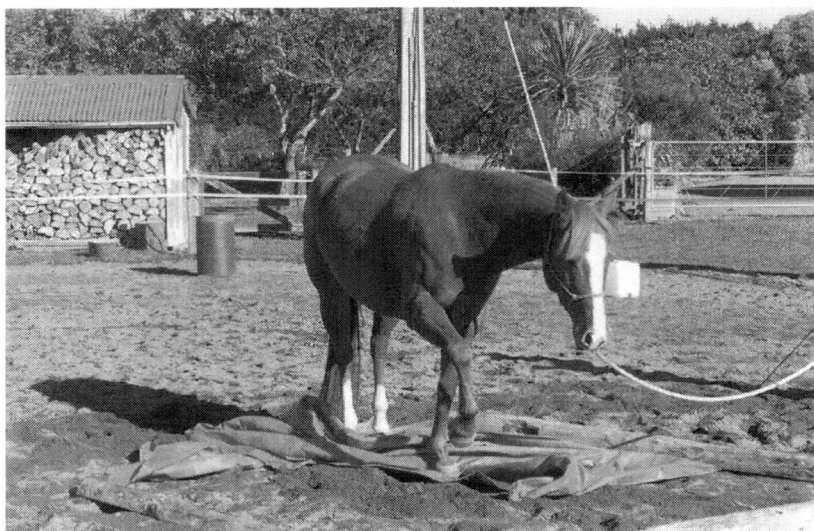

Figure 5: Foot Touch: The first five times I laid out the tarp for Boots to explore, she had a compelling need to paw it into a scrunched ball.

Horses will often paw at soft ground or a puddle to check out whether stepping into it is safe. They often paw when first introduced to a trailer ramp. It is good to be aware of how cautious horses are about where they put their feet.

3. Brief Overview of Signals Types

When I started looking at the specific details that relate to the eight leading positions we use with our horses, I started to think more deeply about how I actually ask my horse to move seamlessly from one position into the next. It had all developed gradually over the thirteen years we've been together.

#26 HorseGym with Boots clip has an overview of the eight leading positions.

Trying to explain the development of the communication to another person is a different kind of challenge.

In order to switch from leading beside the neck/shoulder to walking in front of the horse with our back to him, it is nice to have a clear signal that the horse understands.

In Horse Agility competitions, different obstacles require the handler to guide the horse from different positions. Ground work becomes extremely interesting and full of variety.

Likewise, when we want to move from leading beside the neck/shoulder to a position beside the ribs, and then move to beside the butt and, finally, behind the horse, we need a clear signal for each position.

The key is to create opportunities to play with each position until the horse understands it and is confident with us in that position. We know he is confident when he willingly moves on (or halts) at our request in any of the positions.

Thinking this through led me to look more closely at signals.

3-1: Examples of the Signal Types

Whole Body Language Signals

General Orientations
- Moving from A to B, the horse follows along or moves with us.
- When riding, the rhythm of our body in tune with the gait we are in.
- Facing the horse in front, we can draw him toward us by stepping backwards.
- Facing the horse in front, we can ask him to back up by stepping toward him.
- Facing the horse's ribs, allows us to ask him to move past us or in a circle around us.

Figure 6: Zoe's body orientation is a large part of the signal that she would like Smoky to move over the rails and continue in a circle.

Specific Orientation – the alignment of our body in relation to the horse is a major part of the signal when we ask for:

- weave pattern
- figure 8 pattern
- s-bends (see figure 2), l-bends, u-bends, zigzag-bends
- hindquarter yields
- forequarter yields
- backing up with counter-turns (as in backing a square)
- standing on a mounting block as a signal for the horse to line itself up for mounting

Gesture Body Language Signals

Large: ...sometimes with body extension amplification.

The importance and significance of body extensions are discussed more fully in Part 20. We might sometimes use large body language signals if we are:

- guiding or hazing from behind
- sending the horse away into a frolic

- arm held out as a target to signal a recall.

Medium sized Gestures might be ones we use as:
- back up with hand signals
- 'walk on' signal with arm or outside leg
- facing the horse, hand put up for whoa
- facing the horse, recall signal
- please move sideways away from me
- please move your hip away
- please move your forequarters over.

Small Gestures might include the following:
- walking side-by-side, halt signal by handler dropping into her hips
- hand lightly on poll for 'head down' signal
- hand positioned so horse can target the palm of the hand with his chin
- finger gesture to back up
- stretching out hand, palm down, for horse to touch with his nose; often called the 'horseman's handshake' (see figure 7).

Figure 7: Small Gesture: Bridget and Smoky greeting.

Direct Touch Signals

Hand Touch Only:
- Stroking
- Massage & stretching exercises
- Picking up feet
- Backing up with touch to chest or nose
- Sideways with touch to ribs
- Yield hindquarters with touch to hip
- Yield forequarters with touch to shoulder
- 'Walk on' with finger tap behind withers or on butt

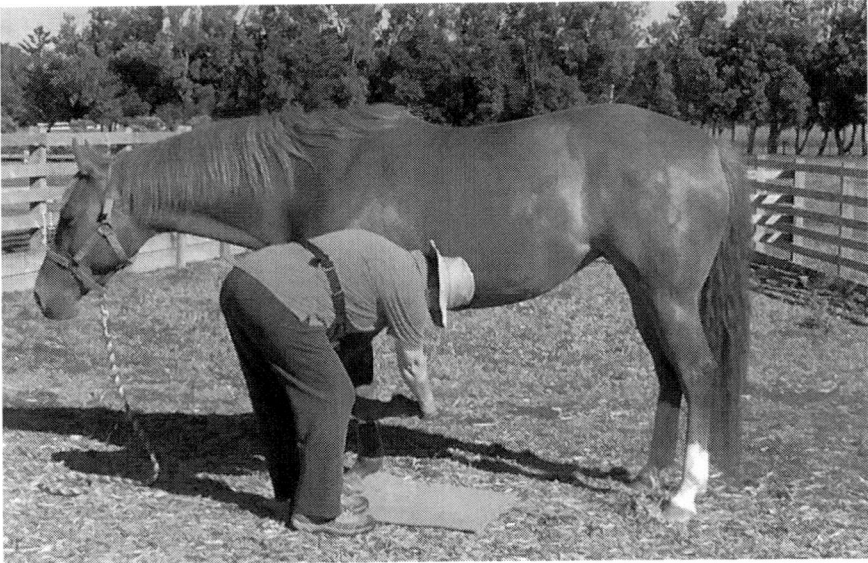

Figure 8: For hoof care, we have to use direct touch signals.

Body Extension Touch include all of the above plus:
- grooming
- cleaning and trimming feet
- head gear put on/off
- ropes all over body
- saddles or harness on/off.

Riding Touch:

Horses are extremely touch-sensitive. They feel every shift of weight and position. As long as we don't desensitize the horse to touch signals by nagging, inconsistency or rudeness, the horse learns to respond to the smallest of touch and weight placement variations.

Head Gear Touch Signals

Via rope while we are working on the ground:
- poll pressure to walk forward
- nose pressure to halt, back-up
- pressure on the side of the head to change direction
- halter vibration to back-up.

Via reins when riding or long-reining:
- nose or bit pressure for change of direction
- nose or bit pressure for downward transitions, halt, back up
- nose or bit pressure to ask for bend.

Figure 9: Riding and long-reining rely on touch signals via the reins to the head gear as well as verbal signals.

Verbal Signals

- "whoa" word or sound
- upward and downward transition words or sounds
- "yes" word along with the release of signal pressure
- If we are using clicker training the marker sound (click) if we are using reward reinforcement (more about clicker training shortly)
- encouraging 'keep going' words or sounds
- inhibiting warning words or sounds

Breathing and body energy

- breath in = raising body energy to prepare to ask for more movement
- breath out = dropping body energy to prepare for slowing down
- large sigh to encourage relaxation
- relaxed posture during relaxation or dwell time between requests

Intent

- how we align the core of our body and our eyes
- how strongly we are focused on what we want to happen
- how we bring our breath and energy up in preparation for giving a signal
- how firmly our inner belief backs up what our signal is requesting

Figure 10: Zoe is using intent & body language to invite Boots across the water.

Marker Signals as used in Clicker Training

A distinct sound or special word is used in Clicker Training which is also called:

- mark & reward training
- positive reinforcement training
- reward reinforcement training.

The special and distinct 'marker' sound lets the horse know when he is offering the required behavior, and it tells him that a treat will immediately follow the click.

It makes the horse pro-active about discovering what it is we want him to do because he is keen to earn the next click and treat. The horse's innate seeking mechanism kicks in and provides natural motivation.

Detailed information about Clicker Training is available in my book: *How to Begin Equine Clicker Training.*

Environmental Signals

- Fresh grass is a powerful environmental signal for most horses.
- Other horses are environmental signals.
- The presence of individual people in the horse's life are environmental signals.
- If we are heading toward a jump or a set of trotting poles, their presence tells the horse that he needs to change his balance to go over the obstacle or navigate around it.
- If we stop at regular spots for rest or grazing when out riding or walking, the horse soon recognizes the spots and expects to stop.
- Other animals are environmental signals, as is the weather and movements caused by the wind.

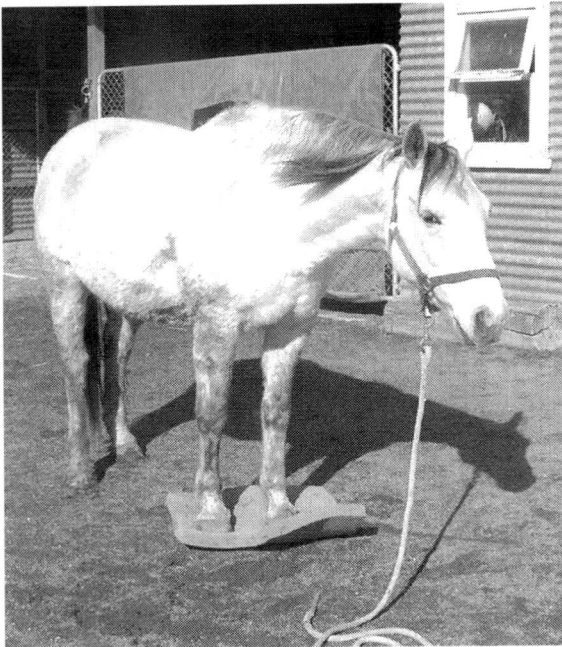

Figure 11: Smoky's long history of reward reinforcement at the mat has made it a desirable environmental destination and he confidently stays there 'ground tied'.

3-2: Signal Bundles or Multi-Signals

Sometimes we use one type of signal in isolation, but often our signal is a mixture of body orientation, body language and gesture, plus body energy change and maybe a verbal component. We are in essence giving 'multi-signals'.

Even if we think we are giving one clear signal, the horse is noticing everything that is happening. That is why it is so easy to inadvertently teach horses things we didn't intend to teach.

We may think we are giving a clear signal but our energy, orientation and intent may not match what we want the signal to say. The horse will always do what he believes to be the right thing to do at that moment.

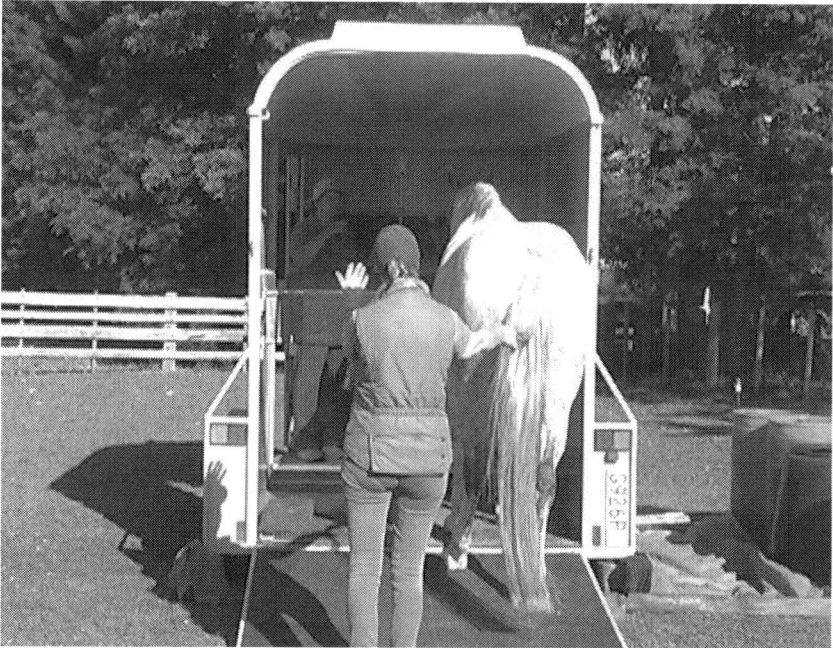

Figure 12: Multi-Signal in action: Bridget is using a touch on the tail, a hand gesture & saying, "Back please" all at the same time.

One reason Clicker Training is so powerful is because it allows us to pinpoint exactly what we want the horse to do. Horses appreciate this clarity enormously. It removes much of the guesswork for them.

The marker signal tells the horse that what he just did is what we wanted and that he can go into treat retrieval mode. The treat is offered right after sounding the marker signal.

We have to remember that body language is a big deal with horses. It is their first language. It helps explain why horses who do marvelous ground work suddenly become 'lost' when their handler mounts up. Suddenly the horse can no longer see all the body language signals that accompany ground work.

Looking at signals in isolation can make it easier to become more mindful about exactly how we are using the orientation of:

- our whole body
- our gestures
- our hands
- our body extensions
- our environment
- our energy
- how and where we present the treat if we are clicker training.

#38 HorseGym with Boots illustrates some of these ideas.

4. Signal Details

By looking at our signals in isolation, we can consider whether:

- we are being clear for the horse
- there is too much 'noise' in our signal
- we need to add something to make our signal clearer
- we can pare down the complexity of our multi-signal
- we should put more energy (intensity) into our signal
- we should put less energy (intensity) into our signal
- our signal duration is too short

- our signal duration is too long
- our timing when we give the signal is 'spot on', 'off' or inconsistent.

We also need to consider the following points.

1. Is our timing when we release the signal pressure (click&treat) good, 'off' or inconsistent?
2. Is the horse in a receptive frame of mind or not? Is he in the right frame of mind to listen and respond, or is his attention elsewhere?
3. Is the horse *mentally* capable of the actions we are requesting, or do we need to divide the task into even thinner 'slices' to make it understandable for him?
4. Is the horse *physically* capable of the actions we are requesting? Have we put in the time and effort to coach the horse with gymnastic exercises? Does he have the muscle tone and strength he needs to carry out a specific request for the duration we are expecting?
5. Is the horse *emotionally* capable of the actions we are requesting? In other words, is something causing him to be reactive rather than responsive?

5. Signal Opportunities

5-1: Noticing our Signal

To begin a conversation with a horse (or anyone) it is important that the other party is not focused on being hungry, thirsty, badly needing to pee or poo, in pain, in a deeply anxious state or needing to attend to a body signal such as itchiness, biting insects, fatigue. Or is the individual bored, disinterested and trying to tune us out?

A horse expressing anxiety, fear or exuberance by wanting to move his feet away from us, is not likely to respond positively to a specific request. Can we wait or change what we are doing until he has used up the adrenalin and is able to connect with us again?

For a high-energy horse, being contained and constrained is often uncomfortable and anxiety-inducing. We can give him the opportunity to use up his adrenalin rush until he feels more comfortable about keeping his feet relatively still. Then we have more chance to make our idea his idea without having to compete so much with the horse's natural resistance to an uncomfortable situation.

Likewise, if the horse is fearful and has mentally shut down and retreated into his private happy place, we need the patience and forbearance to wait for him to re-emerge and re-connect with us in his own time.

When stressful situations arise (which they invariably will) it is helpful, if possible, to set up an environment that allows the horse an opportunity to work through those feelings as safely as possible, in his own time. If we allow the horse the time and space to tune out and then tune in again, we can reward the tuning in and resume two-way communication.

For example, if something in the greater environment causes the horse to go into his fearful mode and he suddenly needs to move his feet, rather than containing him by shortening the rope, we can be prepared by having him on a long rope and allowing him as much of it as he needs.

When he reaches the end of the rope he will turn and the very action of turning momentarily switches his mind from 'flee' to 'assess the situation'.

He may need to run, turn, assess several times (it always seems like ages during the time of an unexpected event) but at some point, he will wonder why he is running and be able to tune in to the handler again.

A safe way to set up the above scenario is to put your back against a safe barrier and allow the horse to move half-circles around you. Reaching the barrier will cause him to pause and think as he turns to run back the other way.

No matter how much we like to gloss up what we do with horses, our intent is for the horse to put his feet where we want them at any particular time. We want him to allow us to make our idea his idea.

We can do that with pressure and releasing the pressure at the 'Yes!" moment. Or we can do it by showing up with a pouch of treats and using reward reinforcement (as with Clicker Training) alongside release reinforcement.

Either way, our basic goal is the same. Reward reinforcement (Clicker Training) makes everything much more enjoyable. However, it has to be learned carefully and done well or problems can arise.

Details can be found in my book, *How to Begin Equine Clicker Training.*

When we are with our horse, we usually make the decision about what we will do next. The clearer we can make our intent using language and signals the horse understands, either innately or through careful education, the more likely the horse will understand what we would like him to do.

Horses are generally co-operative beings. Most horses are happy to comply if the message is clear for them and if what we ask is within their emotional, mental and physical capability.

On the other hand, if we send mumbled or mixed messages or use non-natural signals that the horse has not learned, the horse is in a real bind. A horse in this situation may react in one of the following ways.

1. He may try to fill in with what he thinks the handler might mean, best as he can.
2. He may give up trying to understand and opt out mentally.
3. He may opt out physically by moving his feet to escape the situation, if he can.
4. If he can't escape, he may 'take over' physically by pushing on, through or over the handler.

Choosing the right *opportunity* to ask our horse to do something is important. It's pointless to ask our horse to do something unless there is a 99% chance that he can and will do it. Otherwise we are teaching him to ignore our requests because they are too hard to understand or beyond his physical ability at the moment.

5-2: Setting Up Opportunities

Do we set up lots of occasions for the horse to practice learning what we want him to learn?

In other words, do we give the horse ample opportunity to learn in a controlled environment where he can gradually build his confidence and expand his comfort zone as he comes to understand each new thing we are teaching?

Often people want what they want right now and proceed to demand it with force, coercion and body extensions designed to inflict increasing discomfort.

Since what people want is usually not part of a horse's natural repertoire of behavior, the horse is often catapulted into a state of bewilderment.

How much more comfortable and safer all around, if we thin-slice a large task into its smallest parts, teach each part and then chain the parts together to achieve the whole task?

When we do this, we allow the horse opportunity and time to master each small part before moving on. Please see Parts 8 and 33-5 for more about thin-slicing.

We allow the horse to keep his integrity and goodwill. We allow him to adjust to the strange life he must live with us. We earn his trust so that he is willing to put the placement of his feet into our hands. For an animal, whose sole defense is the ability to flee from perceived danger, this is a big ask.

To build the horse's knowledge and confidence, we need to first get (and reward) the behavior that we want, then we can add a specific signal to it. Often a signal arises naturally out of the way we initiated the behavior.

Once the horse understands that signal, we can layer in other signal types. We can also replace a signal by adding a new one and fading out the earlier one.

Most horses don't seem to have any trouble understanding several signals for the same thing. For example, my horse will 'walk on' with a verbal signal, a 'breath-in' signal, an arm gesture signal and an 'outside leg steps forward' signal. If we are doing work on a long line, she understands the verbal, breathing and arm gesture signals from different angles and distances.

Additionally, horses can understand one signal in a variety of different situations. My horse understands the verbal 'whoa' signal when walking beside me, when she is behind me, when I am walking behind her as in long-reining, and from the riding position.

It's also essential to be aware of the ways that our horse signals to us. Often, we are so immersed in working out what we want the horse to do, we miss the signals the horse is sending us about what he would like us to do, or about his feelings at the moment.

We'll take a closer look at the signals horses use in Parts 30 and 31. The more adept we are at understanding what a horse is trying to tell us, the more accurately we can organize the horse's Individual Education Program (IEP) and adjust it moment to moment as necessary. This is where the term 'reading the horse' is born.

Sometimes, when I sit and read in the paddock, my horse wants to initiate click&treat games, so she comes over and offers me a selection of the things she's learned. If I ignore her, she will gnaw on my chair or gently pull on my jacket to get my attention. Eventually she will relax into grazing or napping near me.

Now let's look in detail at the different types of signals we use with horses.

6. Body Language

We need:
- awareness of our body language
- emotional neutrality
- gear handiness (ropes, reins, body extensions).

6-1: Body Language Awareness

The main tool we have to communicate with our horse is our body language. We instinctively respond to the body language of other people because, like horses, we live in groups. But because people talk so much, we have become less aware of the effect of body language.

Our awareness is still there, but mostly in our subconscious mind. We may reflect on how an interaction with a specific person left us feeling good or not so good. Or we may get a 'gut feeling' about a person on first meeting. In these situations, we are tuning in to our instinctive understanding of human body language.

All species that live in groups need to be able to 'read' each other's body language because the resources of the environment are finite and need to be used by all members of the group.

This means that there is always a subtext of competition for the resources. The less abundant (and the more desirable) any resource is, the stronger the competition for it between members of the group.

A necessary resource in limited supply is called a 'limiting factor'. The sustainable size of a group is determined by such limiting factors. For example, in harsh areas of natural horse habitat, a limiting factor in the winter is food and in the summer access to water within an area that also provides sufficient food.

To prevent energy wastage by constant bickering or fighting within the group, animals that live together have invariably developed sophisticated body language communication.

In human terms, think of posture and intent:

- Shoulders back versus slouched/slumped
- Head high and focused versus head bowed/downcast
- Meeting someone's eye rather than avoiding it
- Standing firm rather than moving away
- Striding purposefully rather than reluctantly
- Chest expanded rather than shrunken/subdued
- Handshake firm rather than limp or aggressive
- Offer handshake rather than wait for the offer
- Approach assertively rather than timidly
- Unsmiling to passer-by versus smiling at passer-by
- Ignore group member versus acknowledging him
- Determined versus dubious
- Confidently neutral versus jittery or nervous

When a teacher and a class of students meet for the first time, the students will have the teacher sized up in the first few seconds of visual contact. Horses are the same. As well as visual signs, people (and horses) give off an aura of energy that spells confidence or anxiety.

Interestingly, with a few adjustments, the body language we already instinctively know and acknowledge in other people can be transferred to our interactions with other group animals such as dogs and horses. On the other hand, it doesn't transfer much at all to solitary-living animals such as cats and bears.

Communication via body language allows two individuals to work out who is senior and who is junior in any encounter – a social order is established. However, a social order is never written in stone. Environment and changing situations can result in a flexible social order, which is probably the case with horses in the wild.

A group member higher in the social order will tend to use the body language on the left of the posture descriptions above and the junior member will tend to use the posture descriptions on the right.

The postures are similar whether we consider people, dogs or horses. A horse willing to touch our outstretched hand with his nose is willingly 'shaking hands'. A dog who rolls over and exposes his belly is volunteering a very timid handshake.

Here are two small horse experiments that could be illuminating. Carry a stick with you, held in neutral. It is there if you need to expand your personal space.

1. Stand in a roomy area or paddock where your horse can see you. Stand very quietly with a slumped and despondent posture. Wait. Observe what your horse does (casually, don't stare at him).
2. While your horse is minding his own business in a roomy area, make your body language large and assertive, focus on him strongly and walk briskly toward his shoulder in a straight line. What happens?

Some people may, without realizing it at first, slip from assertive to aggressive. As with horses and dogs, human aggression often arises from fear and is a defense mechanism, not an attempt to rise up in the social order. This is important to remember when we are around horses.

What looks like aggressive, intimidating horse behavior is often grounded in fear if the horse is contained with ropes or in a small pen. A horse's only way of regaining a feeling of safety is to move himself away as far as he needs to go. When we restrict his ability to move away, his remaining options are limited.

Some people (and some horses) are naturally on the timid end of a 'timid-bold continuum'. A person may want to learn to be assertive with their horse, but quickly slips from assertive to being a wimp. This creates a problem for the horse when he is relying on the person's clear leadership signals, and they are suddenly gone.

Depending on the situation, most people fluctuate between the left and right sides of the posture descriptions on the earlier page. Genetics, past environments and past experiences determine where a person (or a horse or dog) sits most of the time along a timid —— bold continuum.

Around horses, it is important to cultivate the body language on the left side of the descriptions as well as emotional neutrality, which is another crucial tool in our kit.

When forming a relationship with a horse, it is important to become and remain the senior member for two reasons.

1. Our personal safety with a thousand-pound flight animal is easily compromised.
2. Most horses seek leadership. Safety is number one in a horse's psyche. Like us, horses feel safest in familiar company and in a relationship that is clear, consistent, fair and within their understanding.

As group animals, horses are extremely tuned in to body language. The more we can emulate equine ways of socializing and interacting with our body language, the clearer we can become for our horse because we are using his number one language.

More information about Universal Horse Language is available in my book, *How to Create Good Horse Training Plans*.

The strength of the relationship we build with a horse depends on how clearly we can present ourselves to the horse as a senior partner who is confident, trustworthy and fair.

The steps toward this are:
1. *Being accepted as a member of the horse's in-group.* When horses form a social bond with a human, they see the human as a part of their own 'in-group' – a part of their herd. They don't see themselves as belonging to the human's 'in group'.

2. *Earning a standing above the horse in the horse's perception of his social order.* Note this is about the horse's perception, not what we might prefer to think. We find out what his perception is by carefully noting his behavior. If he feels free to push on us to move our feet, bite us or kick at us, then he is not seeing us as a group member senior to himself. He has learned that these behaviors work to remove or divert pressures he does not understand or does not like. Such behavior strongly suggests that he does not see us as a member of his in-group.

3. *Creating willingness in the horse to follow our suggestions.* Clicker Training makes this much more fun for both horse and handler.

These ideas are outlined in detail in my book, *Learn Universal Horse Language.*

6-2: Emotional Neutrality

Our body language is intimately linked with our emotions. The more we can lay aside emotional responses, especially stress-related and negative emotional responses, the more we can be 'in the moment' with our horse. The more we are 'in the moment', the more open we are to picking up the signals the horse is sending us.

The more we can be open to his signals, the better we can 'stay with the horse' and give him time to work out how he can cause the release of the signal pressure (plus earn a treat if we are using Clicker Training).

If we are totally focused on our own agenda, it is hard to also be mindful of the horse's signals and take them on board so we can quickly act in the most appropriate way.

The more negative emotion a horse feels from the handler, the harder it is for the horse to focus on what we are asking. He will either withdraw into himself or seek to escape the situation by looking away and moving his feet away as far as a rope or fence allows.

Emotional neutrality relates to the 'aura of energy' mentioned earlier. A horse can pick up our pleasure and joy when he does something well. He equally picks up every hint of frustration or annoyance. By the time we recognize we are annoyed or angry, the horse will have withdrawn from accepting our leadership at that moment.

It takes a long time to build the trust of a prey animal wired for flight. A moment of aggression can erase a lot of trust. If the horse is contained with rope, reins or small enclosed spaces, he perceives human aggression as a possible attempt to kill and eat him.

Horses don't have a concept of 'punishment'. In a wild herd, a horse always has the option to move away from assertive or aggressive behavior by herd mates. We must never forget that they are prey animals and their key defense is flight.

We have to accept that nothing a horse does is ever a personal affront to us. What a horse does at any one moment is what he feels he needs to do because he is a horse. He may feel he needs to:

1. Stay safe (move his feet to escape, or withdraw into his secret self if he can't get away)
2. Eat (fresh grass is a very strong environmental signal)
3. Tend to a bodily function (pee, poo, itch, rest, swish flies, cool down, rest)
4. Follow our suggestion about what to do next
5. Amuse himself, if he is bored, by moving us around
6. Check out an opportunity to rise in the group social order — challenge our seniority.

Anxious type horses are less inclined to question their position in the social order. They tend to seek leadership and cling to it.

Confident, imaginative type horses tend to seek opportunities to rise in the social order and seem to enjoy testing their humans often to see if they are still worthy of being the leader. It is important to not see this as 'naughtiness', but as a strong-willed horse being his natural self.

More information about Horse Character Types is available in my book, *How to Create Good Horse Training Plans*. You can also access a file link called *PDF Ch 5 Reading Horses* through https://herthamuddyhorse.wordpress.com. When you click 'home', the link is at the end of the first article.

We have taken the horse away from his natural herd situation and put ourselves in place of his horse companions. If he accepts us as a member of his herd, he will behave toward us as he would to another herd member.

That is why it is important to maintain our social position at least one rung above the horse firmly, fairly and consistently.

Conscious development of our own emotional neutrality allows us to respond to the horse as his senior partner, rather than become reactive ourselves when upsets happen.

As we become more aware of what our body language is probably saying to the horse, it becomes much easier to reduce our own anxiety, frustration or fear. Feelings like fear and frustration often lead to aggression or withdrawal on our part.

By 'withdrawal' I mean:
- avoiding spending time with our horse
- losing interest
- deserting our training plans
- reverting to old behaviors that feel familiar

Instead, once we know how, we can try harder to read what our horse is telling us and formulate a new Individual Education Program or tweak our old one.

Individual Education Programs (IEPs) are covered in more detail in my book, *How to Create Good Horse Training Plans*.

As we gain skills of communication and get better at teaching our horse (in a systematic way) our emotional neutrality will last longer and longer. Because horses are super-sensitive to body language and energy aura, they can read our mood in a split second.

People really good with horses have become good because they are observant and empathetic. They have devoted study and time to gain the knowledge and experience needed to make being with horses like second nature.

They know:
- How horses communicate with each other
- When to add pressure to a signal (amplify/advance)
- When to remove pressure (release/retreat/withdraw/click&treat)
- When to wait (give dwell time)
- When to quit a teaching session for the day
- When to just hang out with their horse, sit in the paddock and read or go for a walk together.

People really good with horses have emotional neutrality because they know from experience that what they are doing will lead to the result they want, even though the process looks nothing like the final product. The rest of us get a horse and try to head directly for some final product we visualize in our mind.

The teaching process does not look like the final product.

We all appreciate a companion who is clear, confident and fair. Horses are the same.

7. Signal Timing

Timing is a skill we are always working on because it can always be improved. If we are Clicker Training, the timing of our click, followed promptly by the treat, is crucial.

Unless we are free-shaping a behavior, and therefore not using a signal, the timing of the click will be simultaneous with the timing of the release of our signal pressure.

If we are not using the click&treat dynamic, the only way the horse knows he is doing the 'right' thing is if we release the signal pressure at the instant of the correct response, or as close to a correct response as the horse is able to offer at the moment.

If we want the horse to step backwards with his left front foot, he must first put his weight back and onto his right shoulder so he can physically lift his left front foot. (See *Training Plan 6* in Part 33-10.)

Our first *release point,* if we are using release reinforcement by itself, as we run our hand up the rope toward the halter, would be when we notice that the horse is **thinking** about shifting his weight back.

We feel for that moment when the urge to push forward into the rope pressure changes. That is the instant we need to release the signal pressure (or click&treat as well if we are using reward reinforcement).

The more accurate and consistent our timing, the less bewildered the horse will be as we teach him something new. The more new things he learns really well in a quiet, relaxed manner, the more confidence he will bring to the next challenge we set him.

To carry on with the above example, once the horse understands that a weight shift back earns a release (click&treat), we can withhold the release (click&treat) until he lifts the left foot: release (click&treat). Then we wait for that foot to step back a bit: release (click&treat). Then we wait until the right foot steps back as well: release (click&treat).

Once we have that happening with willingness and confidence, it is easy to build duration to get two full steps, three steps, four steps, five steps and finally as many steps as we want.

In the learning stage, as the horse takes each step back, we 'release' the signal pressure momentarily and then lightly put it on again for the next step, and so on, creating a rhythm.

Once the horse understands the concept and the signal, the energy of our intent and our body language will be enough to keep him stepping backward until we drop the energy of our body (which is a 'release' signal) plus click&treat if we are using reward reinforcement as well.

In other words, we can build the duration of a behavior by fine-tuning the timing of our release (click&treat).

For every movement that we want, there is a sweet spot of balance the horse needs to carry out the movement smoothly. If we want to clean a hoof, we should first stand the horse squarely, so that he can easily shift his balance off the foot we ask for.

If we stop to consider the balance needed before we ask the horse to do something, the timing of our signals will get better and better.

As mentioned above, even more important than the timing of the signal, is the timing of the release of the signal pressure (click&treat).

The signal pressure motivates the horse to do what is correct in our eyes. The release of the signal pressure is what lets him know when he is correct.

If we don't release (click&treat) the instant he is correct, he has no way of knowing what we want.

The other part of this whole equation is to make sure we are teaching in small enough steps or slices so that the horse can be continuously successful with what he is offering.

Here is the excerpt about Thin-Slicing from my book: *How to Begin Equine Clicker Training.*

8. Thin-Slicing Explained

"When we see a horse perform a finished behavior, it is often tempting to try it ourselves, with our horse, by repeating it as we saw it. But that is not how it works.

When we want to train something new, the first step is to experiment a bit to see what the horse can offer already, in relation to the new goal we'd like to achieve.

This will give us an idea of where our Individual Education Program (IEP) needs to start. We want to base it on foundation training (or environmental situations) with which the horse is already confident or at least familiar.

It is also a good way to find any 'training holes' that we need to fill before we enthusiastically head toward setting a new challenge for the horse.

Once we have a starting point, we can begin to write our Individual Education Program by thin-slicing the overall task.

The first step of thin-slicing is a brainstorm to dissect the complete task into its smallest teachable parts. Then we have to organize these components or 'slices' into an order that we think will make sense to our horse.

This becomes the basis of our Individual Education Program (IEP). What makes sense to any particular horse will depend on his innate character type, age, health, fitness and his previous life experiences as well as how we present each new slice of the task.

An Individual Education Program is always a work in progress and usually we go back and tweak it many times. Sometimes we throw the whole thing out and start again.

Each time we work with the horse, we get additional feedback from the horse and from our own reactions and responses.

Thin-slicing means carefully checking (and re-checking) that the horse is comfortable and confident with each tiny slice of the process before we move on. It pays to remember that the *process* of teaching does not look like the finished product.

One horse may learn something in five minutes the first time we teach it. Another horse may take days, weeks or months to reach the same level of confidence and physical expertise.

We have to balance the need to build confidence at each tiny step with the need to move on when we should, so the horse doesn't get bored. It's never easy to walk the fine line between moving too fast and going too slow.

Pacing our training for best results is one of the things that experience, understanding a particular horse's character type, reading the horse carefully and becoming aware of our own body language, will make easier.

When we use this thin-slicing technique, we may find that one horse easily moves through the most basic slices very quickly and we are soon working on more challenging slices.

Every time we start a new task, it's important to not presume we know what the horse already knows. Instead, we should work quietly through the slices in our plan, starting with the most basic requests, until we reach the edge of his comfort zone and slow down at that point. Each horse will have different comfort zone edges.

The next horse we present with the same task may show huge training holes with the most basic slices of the whole task, so we spend more time there.

Since each horse/human partnership is unique, there are no recipes or 'one size fits all'.

Whatever the horse is doing when he feels the *release* and/or hears the *click* is what he will note as the *correct* thing to do in that situation. If our timing is inconsistent, we are making things harder than they need to be – both for ourselves and for the horse.

Timing can be improved with focus and physical practice. Once we can recognize the moments when our timing is off, we can apologize to the horse and strive to do better next time.

It can be fun to practice timing by choosing something specific to 'click' with a clicker, squeeze a soft ball or tap a pencil while watching TV — e.g., every time an actor smiles, or a car comes on screen or the ball reaches the rim of the basket in a basketball game.

If that annoys the person watching with you, get them to do it too! Short, regular bursts of opportunity to do 'timing training' can improve our powers of observation as well as our hand-eye co-ordination many-fold.

9. Signal Intensity

If a horse knows a signal well, it may take only the merest suggestion of it to yield the response we would like. Onlookers will usually not be able to see the signal.

The handler and the horse have developed a secret language that belongs to just the two of them. Each horse and handler combination is totally unique. They will have their own secret language at this level of communication. Maybe it is a bit like the secret language between twins or close friends.

When we first teach a new signal, the energy we put into it may be relatively high at the beginning, until the horse understands what we want. It always depends on the nature of the horse, the specific situation and the relationship (or lack of) already established.

If we are teaching a horse to back up with a touch signal on the halter by running our hand up the rope to the halter until we reach a *point of contact* to which the horse will respond, we may at first have to take a very grounded stance so we can 'hold' against the opposition reflex of the horse, which causes him to push forward.

But as soon as the horse understands that the signal pressure will release if he moves his weight back, the pressure of our next signal can immediately be lighter.

If the horse receives a click&treat as well as release at the 'Yes!' moment, he will soon move back willingly when he reads our body language and intent. We may not even get to the point of running our fingers up the rope.

9-1: Signal pressure can be:

a) Steady

E.g. when teaching the back-up, sliding our hand up the rope to the halter and just 'holding' until the horse shifts his weight and steps back.

b) Gradually increasing

E.g. fingers lightly on chest to ask for back-up and gradually getting a bit firmer until the horse steps back. If we are using reward reinforcement (click&treat) as well, the horse very quickly reads the intent in our body language and often backs up before we even touch him.

As soon as the horse responds, all pressure is removed plus click&treat if we are using reward reinforcement. Sometimes steady pressure is best. For other things, it may be easier for the horse to find the answer we want if the pressure is increasing. Sometimes steady pressure can leave the horse in limbo for too long.

c) Rhythmic

E.g. tapping finger or stick behind the withers to ask for 'walk on please'. The taps can be at a steady pressure or gradually increasing pressure. All pressure stops the moment the horse complies.

d) Rhythmic cyclic

E.g. if the horse doesn't move forward with a light tap behind the withers (or on the butt) we can tap lightly three times and wait briefly, tap slightly harder three times and wait briefly, tap quite hard three times and wait briefly, then return to three light taps and so on, until we get the 'walk forward' response, at which point we instantly stop tapping, (plus click&treat if using reward reinforcement).

This works well because no one wants to keep increasing signal intensity to the point of creating pain. None of the signal pressure we use should give more than discomfort which the horse can stop by moving (or stopping). The horse soon responds to the lightest touch because he knows the pattern of what comes next. He knows how to get us to stop the tapping. We have taught him a life skill.

e) Engage & Remove

E.g. if we are hazing/driving/guiding the horse from behind, we add energy to our body or to our swishy body extensions as a signal to 'move please'. The moment the horse complies, we remove the driving pressure and just follow along. We engage the driving signal energy as needed, and remove it the instant it is not needed, exactly as another horse would do.

9-2: Summarizing Signal Intensity

In the teaching and learning phase, we use the signal intensity we need to allow the horse to understand what we would like it to do; otherwise we are not communicating effectively.

Once the horse understands, it will be reading our body language to find out what signal we plan to give.

It is the same watchfulness they use living in a herd where it pays for them to always know what the horses around them are doing. A carefully educated horse will pick up the first nuance of our signal and respond to that.

In other words, if the horse is tuned in and working with us willingly, our signals can get more and more refined into our 'secret language'.

A: Avoid the Strong Signal Trap

It is easy to get into the trap of always using a high-energy signal because that is what we've always used. Seeing how small we can make a signal is a fun challenge. It makes use of the horse's incredible memory and sensitivity. Often, we shout when we only need to whisper or show our intent through clear, consistent body language.

We especially don't want to get into the habit of nagging by continually repeating an ineffective signal. If it's not getting the response we want, it's not working as a signal. If we keep nagging, we desensitize the horse to our action, which is the exact opposite of what we want.

Some people carry on endless debate about 'steady pressure' versus 'escalating pressure'. In my mind, I don't see a debate. Any of the pressure types described above can be appropriate depending on the horse's Character Type, the specific situation, the horse's previous training and the expertise of the handler.

The skill comes in knowing when to use which one and how to quickly shift from a high intensity signal to the lightest signal possible. A horse can only become as light as we are light with our signal pressure. The horse learns by noting when we remove the signal pressure (click&treat).

In an extreme situation, we may have to momentarily use extreme signal pressure. If the choice is extreme pressure versus injury to us or the horse, it helps to have the knowledge, skill and tools to apply it.

We may only need to use it once in a blue moon, but with horses a dangerous situation can arise any time in totally unpredictable ways.

Some clicker trainers put forward the idea that we can teach almost everything with click & treat (reward reinforcement) only. I don't subscribe to this idea because horses already have a perfectly good first language involving release reinforcement, which is applying and removing pressure.

It makes sense to learn and use this 'first language' before branching out. My book, *Learn Universal Horse Language: No Ropes,* outlines a series of exercises we can use to establish a relationship with a new horse, or consolidate a relationship with a horse we already have.

Handlers new to horses may not understand different Horse Character Types or how to use release reinforcement effectively. They can get themselves into all kinds of bother and danger.

As mentioned earlier, more information about Horse Character Types is available in my book, *How to Create Good Horse Training Plans.*

Many people have a romantic notion about horses which bears little resemblance to the reality of horses. They are captivated by the idea that horses are all-loving, all-knowing and docile if we only ply them with love and food rewards and never push them to do anything they don't want to do.

Sadly, while a person with this vision is figuring out that it might not be true, they can be teaching the horse self-reinforcing avoidance behaviors that will not help him get along in a human dominated life. When that horse gets sold on, he may not end up in a good place.

It makes more sense to marry up the best 'release reinforcement' practices with the immense fun of Clicker Training (reward reinforcement).

Clicker Training is much more than giving the horse an occasional piece of carrot or a rub when he has done a nice job. It's a detailed teaching dynamic that fast-tracks learning by giving the horse motivation that allows him to be pro-active rather than re-active. It engages the very basic seeking part of his brain.

There are several 'layers' to Clicker Training. If you are interested, information is available in my hard copy or e-book called, *How to Begin Equine Clicker Training: Improve Horse-Human Communication*.

B: Appropriate Response to Pressure

Our captive horses live a life full of all kinds of pressures they would never meet in the wild. Even horses kept in groups in huge paddocks or on the range will eventually be faced with small enclosures, halters and ropes.

To cope with this reality, horses need to learn appropriate responses to human pressure. If we fail to teach them, they will not have the total education package they need to remain safe in the large variety of unusual situations they will face.

Ideally, the halter, rope, saddle/harness, reins become positive environmental signals for the horse. Having them on should be similar to a person wearing a uniform for a job they do regularly.

Wearing the uniform brings with it a certain set of behavioral boundaries. When we ask the horse to wear a work uniform, we have to set up careful IEPs (Individual Education Programs) to teach the behavioral boundaries that go with the uniform.

Once the boundaries are well understood, the horse will know how to respond, rather than react, to a range of unusual (for a horse) circumstances.

10. Signal Duration

Duration of the signal will depend on what sort of signal intensity (see Part 9 *Signal Intensity*) we are using and how well the horse knows the signal. Once we are at the 'secret language' stage, the signal might only last part of a second.

Some signals are ON-OFF, such as asking for the 'walk on' around us on a circle. If we nag the horse with a signal for each step, it serves only to make the signal for the transition meaningless.

Other signals work as CONSTANT-ON signals, e.g. asking the horse to move sideways or back-up. We want him to do so until we stop the signal and drop our 'intent' energy.

Some signals are ON-OFF to initiate the movement, followed by a 'background' CONSTANT-ON signal switching in. For example, if we ask the horse to walk beside us, we have a signal for the transition into the walk, then our action of walking signals the horse to keep walking along with us.

Likewise, if we are riding, we use an ON-OFF signal for a transition into trot or canter. Then the rhythm of our body matching the horse's rhythm will be a CONSTANT-ON signal for the horse to stay at that gait.

Figure 13: Once Col has asked Ash to trot, Col's body energy will be Ash's signal to keep on trotting.

If our body movement doesn't fluidly follow the movement of the horse's gait, it is both confusing and uncomfortable for the horse.

When we want to make a downward transition, we reduce the energy of our body and change our body rhythm to the slower gait. Used consistently, the change in energy and rhythm will themselves be the only signals the horse needs to adjust his balance and gait. This is true for riding and ground work.

11. Parameters

Once we appreciate the sensitivity of horses, we can appreciate how sensitive we need to become about the way we apply our signals. It is often said that, "Everything means something to a horse," or "Nothing means nothing to a horse". That is hard to deny and is probably true for all prey species.

We tend to forget, looking at our horses in captivity, that we can take the horse out of the wild, but the wild remains in the horse.

People generally breed from horses with more manageable and less flighty natures, but a few thousand years is a short time in evolutionary history. Horses are as wired for constant awareness as are squirrels on the lookout for cats, dogs, weasels, hawks and snakes.

Before looking in detail at the types of signals we use, let's stop for a moment and look at the way we need to manage parameters when we are teaching a desired behavior.

A 'parameter' is something that we are keeping constant.

If we want to educate our horse to walk beside us politely when we are leading him, we might start with a laneway and ask the horse to walk through the lane while we walk on the outside of the lane. We are using the lane as an environmental signal.

#39 & #40 HorseGym with Boots illustrate the use of lanes.

We could start with a lane made of raised rails (or a fence on one side and raised rails on the other side. This helps keep the horse straight and avoids creating the habit of shifting his hind end sideways, or running his shoulder into the handler.

1.   Walking beside the horse, staying on the outside of the lane, we ask him to walk through the high-sided laneway. That would be our first parameter.
2.   If we then ask him to halt in the center of the lane, wait a second, then carry on walking through, we have changed a parameter.
3.   If we ask him to halt in the lane and wait for three seconds instead of one second, we have changed a parameter. We can change this 'duration' parameter second by second until the horse can halt and wait confidently for as long as we want.
4.   If we walk the horse into the lane, halt, pause, then back out of the lane as we walk backwards with him, we have changed a parameter.
5.   If, instead of walking backwards as he backs out, we turn so we can walk forward while he is backing, we have changed a parameter.

6. If we walk him into the lane, halt, then move from beside him to stand inside the lane facing him so we can ask him to back out of the lane using a different signal, we have changed a major parameter.
7. If we keep a high rail on one side but lower the rail on the other side, we have changed a parameter.
8. If we repeat the exercises with two low rails, we have changed a parameter.
9. If we repeat the exercises with two rails on the ground, we have changed a parameter.
10. If we repeat the exercise with one rail between us and the horse, we have changed a parameter.
11. If we repeat the exercise with one rail on the far side of the horse, we have changed a parameter.
12. If we repeat the exercise with a fence on the far side of the horse, we have changed a parameter.
13. If we repeat the exercise with no rails, we have changed a parameter.
14. If we repeat the exercise in a new venue, we have changed a parameter.

Whenever we change a parameter, we return to releasing (click&treat) for 'less' and work our way forward again until the horse can confidently get 10/10 in the new situation.

Horses are super observant of such small changes, and can often be 'thrown' by them if we proceed too fast or ask for too much too soon.

By 'thrown', I mean that the horse has a loss of confidence. It may be only a small loss quickly remedied. But it could also be a major loss causing the horse to shut down or move his feet in a desire to escape the situation.

The solution is always to back up in the Individual Education Program (IEP) to a point where confidence returns, and work forward again from that point.

Toward the end of the book, there are eight Training Plans that can be used as springboards to create IEPs for individual horses.

People who are good with horses tend to focus on the following points.

- They have become aware of their own body language.
- They can read the horse's body language – not just the big things, but the small nuances particular to each individual horse.
- They recognize a variety of innate Horse Character Types – not much different from what we observe in humans – and develop strategies that work best for each type.
- They expect horses to act differently in different locations, different situations and with different handlers.
- They allow adjustment time for a horse faced with a new venue and/or a new handler.
- They appreciate that tame horses see us as part of their herd and form very close bonds with favorite people, just as they do with favorite horse friends.
- They understand that the sheer size of horses means that there is always an element of possible unintended physical injury caused by the horse's startle response.
- They understand that being part of a horse's in-group means maintaining a standing in the group social order at least a step higher than the horse.

As we gain experience with horse sensitivity, our own body orientation and the signals we are using, we will get better and better at being aware of which parameters we are setting and when we change them. This is an integral part of thin-slicing large tasks into their smallest teachable parts. (Please refer back to Part 8: *Thin-Slicing Explained*.)

12. Rules Work in Both Directions

We can think of parameters as 'the rules of the game'. It is up to us to teach the horse the rules of the game we want to play with him. Equally, it is up to us to stay true to the rules.

The horse can only become as reliable as we are reliable in our teaching.

Everything we want to do with horses entail having control of where the horse puts or keeps his feet.

We can then add other things to go with this 'foot control': things like wearing a saddle, carrying a rider, specific body flexions and particular ways of moving his feet.

To teach the rules of the game fairly, the handler needs to be aware of the following points that underpin all training.

- What thin-slices do I needed in order to teach the overall task to a particular horse?
- How little or how much does this horse already understand about the task?
- What gaps are there in my gear handling and training skills?
- How am I orientating my body in relation to the horse (at all times)?
- How consistent are my signals?
- How good is the timing of my release (click&treat)?
- How good and consistent are my rope handling skills?
- How well and consistently do I handle my body extensions (including rope/reins)?
- How good am I at using my breathing and core body energy to show intent?

The horse can only be as smooth as the handler is smooth. The horse can only learn as smoothly as we can teach smoothly.

Becoming aware of when we change a parameter (causing the unconscious changes to become conscious) is a big step forward as we develop our skill.

13. Signal Type - General Orientation

Since horses notice everything (being so much more aware than we are), where we are standing or moving in relation to the horse has a great deal of meaning for him unless he has learned to ignore it because his humans are inconsistent.

This realization got me started looking with interest at the positions we use for leading or directing horses. I found that we use Eight Leading Positions (see Part 28, *Example 4*).

An overview of these Eight Leading Positions can be found in *#26 HorseGym with Boots*. The book I went on to write is called *Walking with Horses: The Eight Leading Positions.*

After working through Leading Position Three (beside neck or shoulder) I realized that in order to explain how I had taught my horse to move into and out of the various leading positions, I had to take a very close look at the signals we were using.

My horse and I have developed our 'secret language', over many years, in an organic way. To explain it to another person was going to take more than a five-minute video clip.

The various orientations include:
1. beside the neck/shoulder on right side, facing forward
2. beside the neck/shoulder on left side, facing forward
3. beside the neck/shoulder on right side, facing backwards
4. beside the neck/shoulder on left side, facing backwards
5. beside the neck/shoulder on right side, facing the horse's neck/shoulder
6. beside the neck/shoulder on left side, facing the horse's neck/shoulder
7. beside the ribs, right side, facing forward
8. beside the ribs, left side, facing forward
9. beside the ribs, right side, facing backwards
10. beside the ribs, left side, facing backwards
11. beside the ribs, right side, facing the ribs
12. beside the ribs, left side, facing the ribs
13. beside the butt, right side, facing forward

14. beside the butt, left side, facing forward
15. beside the butt, right side, facing backwards
16. beside the butt, left side, facing backwards
17. beside the butt, right side, facing the butt
18. beside the butt, left side, facing the butt
19. behind the horse slightly to the right side, facing forward
20. behind the horse slightly to the left side, facing forward
21. right behind the horse (which is a major 'blind spot' for the horse), facing forward
22. right in front of the horse facing him (ideally beyond his blind spot)
23. in front of the horse, facing him, a bit to his left
24. in front of the horse, facing him, a bit to his right
25. right in front of the horse facing away from him (many people lead this way)
26. in front of the horse, facing away from him, a bit to the left
27. in front of the horse, facing away from him, a bit to the right.

So, we have a minimum of 27 body positions we can adopt when we are doing things with our horse on the ground. The list doesn't include all the angle variations. It also doesn't include all the adjustments we make when we are grooming or tending the feet.

Whether the horse is standing still or we are in motion together, the orientation of our body is part of the message we are sending the horse at any one moment.

It's hard for us to realize how sensitive horses are to position. In many cases our lack of awareness of our position has taught the horse to ignore much of what we do.

Recently I taught my horse to activate individual feet by pointing at them (at the halt).

I consistently use the arm furthest from the horse to signal, "Please lift hind leg nearest me". I use the arm nearest the horse to signal, "Please lift the far hind leg". To make it clearer, I tilt my head away from the horse for the near hind leg and toward the horse to ask for lifting of the far hind leg. It is getting better and better and saves me having to walk around the horse to activate the far hind leg. Using click&treat makes it a fun game for both of us. *#66 HorseGym with Boots* illustrates what we were doing.

14. Signal Type - Specific Orientations

The way we use our body, if we are consistent in our movements, can make it much easier for the horse to read our 'intent'. As mentioned earlier, body language expressing 'intent' is the main natural communication system between horses.

Example 1. If I want to teach the horse to weave a series of markers, I ask him to 'drive' away from me around one marker, then 'draw' toward me for the next one, then 'drive' away from me for the next, and so on.

- To signal the horse I use a slight lean toward him for the 'drive' signal and a slight lean away from him for the 'draw' signal.

- At first I accentuate my 'lean' with actual movement toward and away from the horse. During the teaching phase I also gesture with a body extension or an arm/finger movement.

- As the horse gets to understand the pattern, I gradually reduce the body language to a tilt of my head toward or away from the horse.

- Even more refined, the horse will respond to simple body orientation (toward or away).

- The timing of the signal is important. As the horse comes around one marker, we have to be ready with our signal to set him up for the next marker.

Example 2. If I want the horse to move his hind end away when I look at it with focus and strong intent,

- I begin with strong focus on his hip, slightly leaning toward it.
- Then tap the ground with a body extension.
- If there is no response, I tap or tag the horse's flank until there is a response. Which option I would use (tag or tap) depends on the character type of the horse, where we are in our training and the nature of the specific situation.
- The moment he responds, I stand up from the slight lean and remove the energy of my intent (plus click&treat if I am using that).
- As the horse gains understanding of my body language, and as long as I keep the movement fresh in our repertoire, the intense focus toward his quarters will be enough to get the response.

Example 3. Walking directly toward the front of the horse in a relaxed manner with my hand outstretched, palm down (to stand in for another horse's nose) shows my intent to offer a greeting (see figure 7).

It resembles the touch of 'noses' between individual herd members known to each other. This way of approaching a horse is often called the 'horseman's handshake'.

Example 4. Walking toward the horse's side behind the *drive line* with strong intent and body extensions (activated as needed), communicates that I want the horse to move away.

The *drive line* is at the base of the horse's neck. Pressure in front of the drive line causes the horse to slow down or turn away. Pressure behind the drive line causes the horse to speed up, yield the hindquarters or move sideways.

These are all natural horse body language signals that horses who have grown up with other horses innately understand. If we use these signals clearly and consistently, horses recognize them easily despite the strange vertical shape of our human body.

15. Signal Type - Gestures

Depending on the situation, our gestures might be large, sustained and supported with body extensions, or they might be very small and last only a moment.

A gesture can be an on-off signal. We ask for 'walk on' with an arm movement, then return our arm to 'neutral'. We want the horse to keep walking until we give another signal. If we are walking with the horse, our whole-body language as we walk along will be a 'keep going' signal.

Alternately, we may want to give an on-off 'walk on' signal while we stand still and ask the horse to walk a circle around us, taking responsibility for maintaining the walk until we request an upward or downward transition.

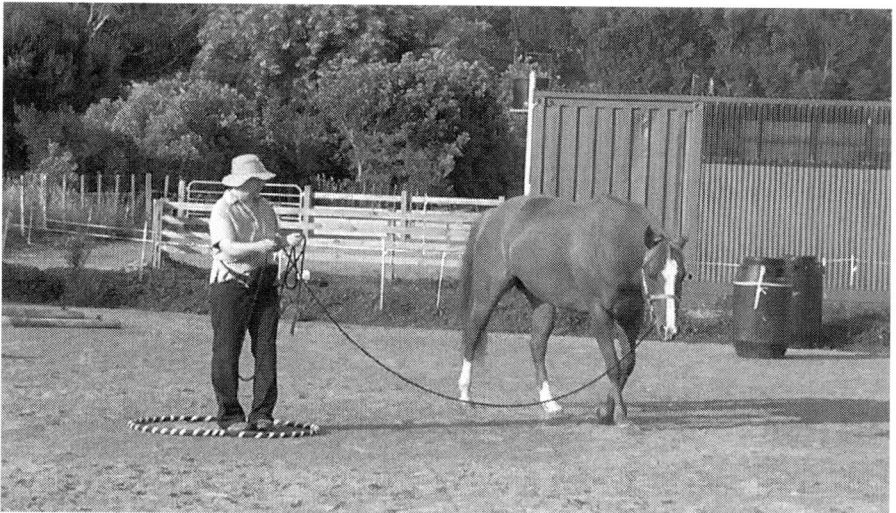

Figure 14: On-Off Signal: After asking the horse to 'walk on', we want him to carry on walking until we give another signal.

Some gesture signals will 'stay on' for the duration of the movement that we want. If we are asking for a turn on the haunches, we will keep the gesture and body language turned on rhythmically until we have the number of steps we want. The removal of the gesture signal becomes a signal to the horse that he should stop.

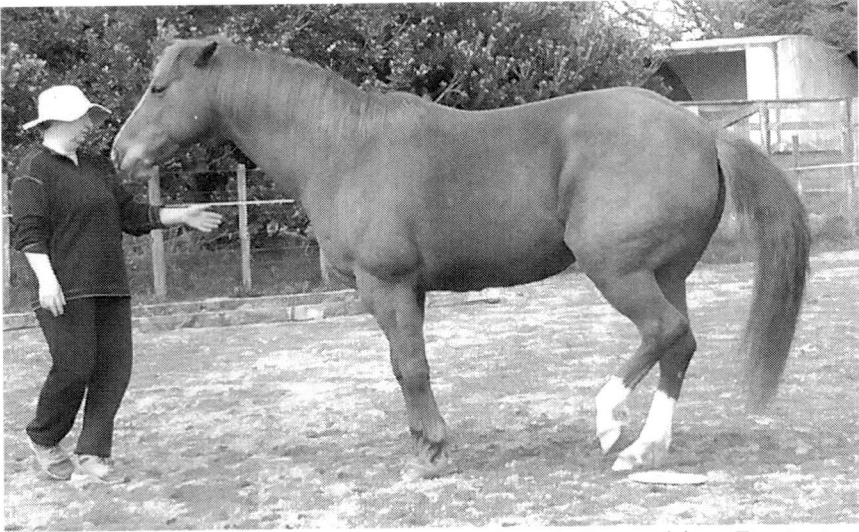

Figure 15: Constant On gesture signal: I'm asking Boots to place her left hind foot onto the 12" disc. I will keep the signal 'on' rhythmically until her foot lands on it.

Gestures can be static (holding out a hand so the horse can target it with a body part) or they can be moving, like wiggling the fingers up at eye level for a back-up while in the 'shoulder-to-shoulder' position.

They can be rhythmic like my hand signal in figure 15 asking Boots to target the 12" disc with her left hind foot.

Most often we gesture with our hands and arms, but we can use our legs if we are asking the horse to back up if he is walking right behind us.

We can also drop our head as a signal for the horse to drop his head. See the two YouTube video clips about *Head Lowering* in my *Free-Shaping* playlist.

However, we need to be careful what we teach and how we teach it. If we teach head lowering by modelling it, the horse may read our dropped head as a signal, when all we want to do is check our footing, look at our shoes, or lean down to pick up the rope.

A large part of horse gesture language involves their ears and tail. If we use a stick&string combination body extension, we can emulate tail signals by the way we move the string — all without touching the horse. We can put a great deal of finesse into how much or how little we 'twitch' the string. Horses notice everything.

Emulating ears is a bit harder, but it's probable that horses read the intensity or relaxation of our facial expressions or the aura that accompanies those.

16. Touch Categories

Here are some categories we can use to differentiate different kinds of touching.

A: Standing Touch

Standing touch is one that does not require the horse to move. It is a touch that we would like the horse to enjoy or tolerate with confidence.

Many of these touches are well outside a horse's comfort zone. Other than mare and foal interactions, horseplay among youngsters, mutual grooming, dominance procedures and fighting, there is not a lot of touching in horse society.

We want our horses to stand still for:
- rubbing, scratching
- grooming
- foot care
- massage, Bowen treatment
- dealing with halters, bridles, covers, saddles, harness
- vet care procedures
- worming
- mounting and dismounting
- tying up.

Because these are life skills every domestic horse needs, it is important to write careful Individual Education Programs to build the horse's confidence with each one.

The key element is relaxation. Although we should be able to tie up our horse, a well-educated horse in his home environment should not need to be tied up. We need to be able to do most of the above with the lead rope dropped to the ground.

Figure 16: Bob is confident with 'standing touch' as he enjoys a neck massage with Lorraine.

Standing still for mounting and dismounting are key elements in the education of a riding horse. We can make it easier for the horse by progressing in tiny steps (slices) that allow him to be comfortable with each part of the mounting and dismounting processes.

Asking horses to stand still when their instinct tells them to move away is a huge part of the training needed to help horses cope in the human centric world they find themselves in. *#20 HorseGym with Boots* looks at the art of standing still.

B: Needing a Balance Shift:

Examples of a balance shift:
- asking the horse to lift a leg for foot care
- when riding, we use touch for most of our signals and the horse has to maintain his balance in relation to the balance (or imbalance) of the rider

C: Please Move Away from this Touch:

Examples of moving away from our touch:
- backing with hand on nose or chest
- yielding quarters, yielding sideways
- tap behind withers or on butt to step forward
- hands on cheeks for head rocking
- touch on poll to drop head
- wiggle energy on the halter, via the rope, to back up

D: Please Follow the Feel of this Touch:

Examples of following the touch:
- rope or rein signal pressure on the head gear
- gentle backward pull signal on the tail
- leading with a signal to the ear, cheek or chin
- holding the tongue

Figure 17: Zoe's gentle pressure on the halter (and her body language) give Boots the signal to step down off the pedestal.

E: Please Move to Initiate this Touch (Targeting):

'Please move so you can touch this' is called 'targeting'. It is usually taught with reward reinforcement (Clicker Training). We can teach the horse to target objects in our hand, put his nose on environmental objects or put his feet on a mat or pedestal.

We can also teach him to target various body parts to our hand.

Examples of the horse initiating the touch:

- target nose to our hand or hand-held target object
- target nose to environmental object like a post or rock or tree or tractor or rags/plastic bottles tied up for the purpose of creating destinations for the horse
- target foot to a mat
- target chin to our hand
- target ear to our hand
- target knee to our hand

- target shoulder to our hand
- target ribs to our hand
- target hip to our hand
- target forehead to our hand
- ring bell by nuzzling with lips
- pick up objects

17. Signal Type - Direct Touch Generally

As mentioned earlier, direct touch is not common among horses. Once a foal is weaned, he will play dominance games with other youngsters. Buddies in a herd occasionally groom each other. Herd members stand head-to-tail and swish flies off each other.

Stallions connect with each when they have physical confrontations. Stallions and mares consort for mating. Mares bite each other and youngsters to sort out and maintain social order. But in an established herd, most communication is by the flick of an ear, a gesture with the neck, and general body language.

Other than these few occurrences, touch does not play a huge role in a horse's natural life. When we come along and want to rub all over them, take liberties with their faces, pull on ropes, fling on covers and saddles, it helps to realize these are foreign concepts to the horse.

The old idea of tying a horse to a post and 'sacking him out' was a rather crude way of flooding the horse's sensibilities until he submitted to these indecencies by giving up the struggle to get away.

We still need our domestic horse to submit to these things, but we can develop Training Plans that take into account how the horse feels.

Anything we want to teach can be thin-sliced into portions tiny enough so the horse can learn that each 'slice' is harmless. We allow the horse to become confident with them one at a time and eventually chain them all together to achieve the overall task.

It seems that some horses come to enjoy being touched and groomed and draped over. Others, not so much.

Horses will tolerate touch and the discomforts of saddles and riders once they have become habituated, but may object to poor-fitting gear in a variety of ways.

Objections may be subtle and not noticed by the handler. If objections are noticed, they are often ignored or the horse is blamed for being 'annoying' or 'bad'.

Frequently horses trying to communicate their objections are handled with more severe equipment or put under greater restraints.

Objections due to pain or discomfort may show up as:
- cinchiness, unhappy with the girthing process
- avoiding being caught
- general unease or lack of confidence under saddle or harness,
- objecting to foot care procedures
- not standing relaxed for grooming
- bucking
- rushing
- running away
- not wanting to leave home area.

Since it is inevitable that horses will have to deal with head gear, ropes and reins, teaching 'Rope Relaxation' is a key element of getting a horse confident with direct touch.

The rope is a body extension. We need to take the time and make the effort to build the horse's confidence with having all sorts of body extensions tossed over him or rubbed over him.

A horse not confident with these procedures will have safety issues.

Video clip #22 *HorseGym with Boots* has more information about *Rope Relaxation*.

18. Signal Type - Hand Touch

We use our hands (and legs if riding) to give a large variety of direct touch signals. Some of these are:

- stroking
- massaging
- lifting feet
- backing up with touch on the nose
- backing up with touch on the chest
- hindquarter yields with touch on the hip (leg toward the hip if riding)
- forequarter yields with touch on the shoulder (leg toward the shoulder if riding)
- stepping sideways with hand touch on the ribs (leg if riding)
- tap behind the withers as a 'walk on' signal
- tap on butt as 'walk on' signal
- pull-touch on tail as a 'back-up' signal
- touch on poll for head lowering
- touch on cheeks for 'head rocking'
- touch on gum to insert bit
- touch of arm across mane to put on halter

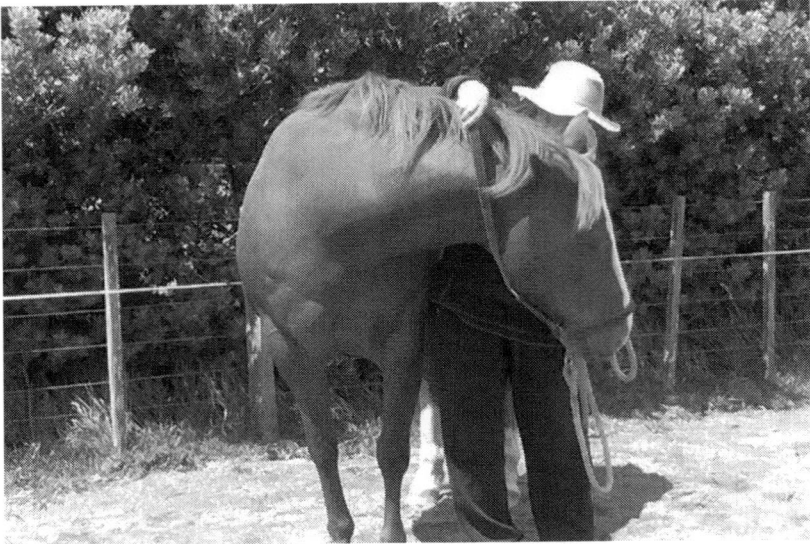

Figure 18: Direct Touch: to hold the halter open so Boots can offer to put her nose into it, she has to be confident with the touch of my arm across her neck.

19. Signal Type - Riding Touch

If we are riding, our balance directly affects the horse's balance. The horse can feel everything. A horse started under saddle thoughtfully will have been given the opportunity and time to re-calibrate his balance with the rider at all of the gaits.

It helps if the horse is encouraged/allowed (depending on character type of horse) to move forward freely to find his new sweet spot of relaxation when carrying the burden on his back.

If we hold off riding until after the horse has learned a variety of halter touch signals as part of ground work it is easier for him to process the new experience of a rider aboard.

His confidence with this unusual and unnatural situation will improve rapidly if he has consistently positive experiences.

If he is not improving, chances are that one or more of the following are involved:

- the riding gear may be causing pain
- the horse is extra sensitive to an unstable rider
- past trauma with a rider causing deep anxiety
- the horse has a muscular-skeletal problem causing discomfort/pain/agony.

Horses can be trained to compensate for rider weight shifts. Think of circus horses, the tricks performed in Cavalia, the way American First Nation people could hang on the far side of a horse to approach bison, and the horses used with Riding for the Disabled programs.

Often people throw a whole lot of new learning at a horse and wonder why he flounders. Professional trainers who work to a time = results = payment schedule can put a veneer of performance on a horse, but there is no substance or solid foundation underneath it.

Often what the horse has learned is not readily transferable to the owner who has a different manner, different signals and a whole different way of doing things.

Additionally, horses sent elsewhere for 'training' are seldom given enough time to feel emotionally 'at home' in the new place. Their learning, rather than optimal, is often pushed on top of the feelings of insecurity and anxiety from being in a new and strange environment.

Just as they are starting to feel more at home, they get sent back or sold on to yet another home. This is emotionally difficult for horses because by nature they need to belong to a stable social group.

20. Signal Type - Equipment Touch and Body Extensions

We can use equipment to amplify the touch we give with our hand, change the nature of the touch or apply the touch from further away and therefore in a greater variety of body positions and body orientations.

People use an interesting variety of equipment:
- grooming gear including clippers
- hoof picks, rasps, hoof knife, nippers
- tooth care equipment
- halters & ropes
- lunge lines
- bridles & reins
- harness/cart & long reins
- covers
- saddle pads and saddles
- body extensions.

Horses are not worried about the items themselves. But they can certainly become worried if the items are not introduced politely and progressively in a confidence-building way.

Horses will become anxious about any pressure that is not withdrawn the instant the horse complies with what he thinks the request was. If gear becomes associated with pain or an initial emotive fear response, we have caused ourselves and our horse a problem we didn't have before.

More about Body Extensions

Again, horses are not worried about any stick we may carry. They have their own set of body extensions in the form of neck, head, legs and tail. But as mentioned earlier, they can certainly become worried if the stick pressure is not withdrawn the instant the horse feels he has complied with the request that was made.

If the pressure is not removed at the precise moment the horse is doing what we want, he has no way of knowing what it is that we want.

If the pressure is not removed, the horse usually experiments with a series of responses. If that does not bring relief, he generally panics and switches from responsive move into reactive mode, which means he feels the need to move his feet away from the situation.

Some introverted horses will 'shut down' and temporarily retreat emotionally into a protective 'happy place'. It is important to recognize the difference between a confident relaxed horse and a 'shut down' horse who is quiet but certainly not relaxed.

The 'stick' has gathered an interesting set of names over the last few years, with the advent of natural horsemanship. We might now be using: sticks, dressage whips, lunging whips, driving whips, wands, swishy twigs, training sticks, arm extensions, reeds, stick&string combinations, Carrot Sticks™.

I like to give them a generic name of Body Extensions, BEX for short. It's worth talking a little bit more about body extensions.

Horses are the shape of a long rectangle. Their neck and legs are their personal body extensions which they use to send a variety of signals to herd mates. People, on the other hand, are the shape of an upright tree and therefore present a curiosity to a horse trying to understand our meaning.

By using a stick extension of some kind, we can become clearer for the horse. Carrying a stick and using it with finesse narrows the comprehension gap when it comes to communicating with body language. Additionally, if the unexpected happens, a stick allows us to protect our personal space bubble without striking out toward the horse.

The biggest deterrent to making 'every horse day a good horse day' is the quite natural fear people have about getting hurt.

Whether the fear is on the surface or a residual fear from scary happenings in the past, it throws a damper over the whole horse-human interaction.

If we are twitchy, the horse will be twitchy. If we are calm and relaxed, the horse has a chance to be calm and relaxed.

So, carrying a stick of some sort, or a piece of string that can be activated like a helicopter blade if the need to protect ourselves arises, can keep us feeling safe every time we are with our horse.

We may rarely need to activate our body extension as a safety device. If we learn to carry the stick in neutral and use it to accentuate or clarify our signals, the horse will see it as our natural body extension, just as he appreciates the ears, neck, leg and tail extensions of another horse's body.

Body extensions can become a problem in some situations.

- A big problem results if they turn into punishment tools which cause the horse to be afraid. Using a body extension to protect one's own space is totally different from using a body extension to intrude into the horse's personal space. Horses read action and the intent very accurately. Using a body extension to defend our own personal space is the same as the martial arts concept of self-defense, as opposed to aggression toward the other party.

- A body extension can become problematic if it is not used as part of a signal in a *consistent* manner that allows the horse to understand its purpose.

- It can become a problem if the signals the horse receives are contradictory. Whip pressure to move forward along with rein or rope pressure inhibiting forward movement is sadly a very common example when the rider is fearful.

Used thoughtfully, carrying a body extension is a win-win situation. The horse recognizes our extensions as part of us. We know we can protect our personal space if the need arises.

Even the most docile and well behaved horse can have a startle response or become super active with an adrenalin rush. If a horse sees us as his point of safety, natural horse behavior causes him to push into the middle of the herd, which will be on top of us.

When the horse considers us to be a herd mate, he expects us to be as robust as another horse. It pays to be prepared. Accidents happen in the blink of an eye.

Figure 19: Carrying a body extension: Bridget is in relaxed mode while Smoky walks a circle. Her body extension is in neutral. She uses it only as needed to clarify her signals.

21. Signal Type – Head-Gear Touch

Sometimes we are so used to doing or seeing something done, that we seldom stop to think about it.

When we slip a halter on a horse and attach a rope, we are changing his whole life while it is on.

Rather than making his own decisions about where he will put his feet, the horse suddenly has his head held captive by a foreign species and is expected to understand what to do.

So it is important to provide the horse with:

- teaching in a way that allows the horse to understand each part of the process (*acquisition*)
- the opportunity to practice what we would like him to know, allowing the time an individual horse needs to absorb the new learning (*fluency*)
- the opportunity to take the new learning from the safe learning environment to other places (generalization).

21-1: Touch via Rope with ground work

Touch pressure on head gear during ground work includes:
- poll pressure to move forward or put head down
- nose pressure to slow, halt, back-up
- pressure on the side of the head for change of direction or neck flexion
- whole halter vibration for backing up
- rope/halter pressure to bring head up from grass.

A horse that understands all these pressures and complies willingly is light to lead forward, light to back up and light to change direction. We have to take the time and trouble to teach these life skills well.

Training Plan 5, *Rope Texting* in Part 33-9 looks at how we can learn to handle a lead rope so it is a soft, positive communication channel between our hands and the horse. The finesse we learn with the lead rope on the ground transfers directly to the finesse with which we can handle the reins when we ride or long-rein.

Clicker Training allows horses to learn faster because it lets the horse know the precise moment he is doing what we want. However, we don't want to forever click&treat the horse for basic foundation work. Once a life skill becomes a strongly set habit, we gradually decrease the click&treat frequency and gradually phase it out for most things.

The release of the signal pressure will still give the horse feedback that he is correct. Click&treat can still be used occasionally for an excellent effort or a general 'thank you'. The click&treat can be replaced by an expression of joy at a YES! moment. Horses seem very tuned in to happy vibes coming from their people.

They are equally tuned in to negative, angry, frustrated, fearful or contradictory vibes coming from their people. If we lose our emotional neutrality when we are with our horse, it is best to stop what we are doing until we have regained it, had a think and a close look at our horse's Individual Education Program.

See Part 26 for a bit more information about Clicker Training.

My book, *How to Begin Equine Clicker Training: Improving Horse-Human Communication* is available as hard copy or e-book.

21-2: Touch via Reins

When we ride, most of our body suddenly disappears from the horse's vision. For an animal whose main language is reading body language, this is a big deal.

Lots of people have a wonderful ground work relationship, but hit snags as soon as they start to ride. Since the horse can no longer read the person's total body language, body orientation, and gesture signals, he is suddenly left rudderless.

We have to take the horse through a careful teaching schedule so he can learn the new way we will communicate with him when we ride. We can teach things like response to gentle rein signals from behind the drive line before mounting up.

We can do this by standing on a safe pedestal beside the horse's ribs and activating the reins from behind the withers. The process is illustrated in my *Developing Soft Rein Response* playlist (5 short clips).

The most educational way to get a feel for using ropes and reins is to have a person hold the halter in their hands and tell you what they feel as you ask them to do a variety of movements with rope signals only.

Even more educational is to stand in for the horse yourself. Have a selection of people ask you to do ground games or long-rein you around a course of objects and obstacles. It won't take long to work out which people you would rather have in your life as a horse.

Figure 20: Be the horse: By holding the halter in our hands we can 'become' the horse and find out how communication through the rope feels.

Teaching long-reining is a fun way to put 'guiding from behind' into practice. The horse can know all about rein pressures for downward transitions, changes of direction, halts and back-ups before he has to learn to adjust his balance with the rider aboard.

Once the rider is up, the horse still has to learn the meaning of the new body touch signals the rider will give (consciously and unconsciously) when riding.

A DVD & Notes set about teaching long-reining is mentioned in the Further Resources section at the end of the book.

Figure 21: Long-reining Boots on the farm. Going to new places is part of the 'generalization' of a new skill. Please see Part 32-4 for more information about 'generalization'.

22. Signal Type – Verbal

22-1: Equine Verbal Signals

Let's look first at the sounds that horses use. They don't have a lot of verbal signals but there are some.

- **Soft nicker** to a foal or friend. It's nice to use this nicker sound if we are approaching a horse when he seems asleep, in the dark or from a position where he can't see us.
- **Sigh** as a strong release of breath the horse has been holding in due to tension resulting from fear or confusion, or to release tension after prolonged focus. Often, we can encourage a horse to 'breathe out' by modelling some big 'sighs' ourselves.

- **Chortle**, which sounds like it is part blowing out air through the nose and adding a deep tone from the vocal cords. It's often part of a greeting. Some clicker trained horses seem to use it as an expression of enjoyment and togetherness.
- **Releasing Snort**, which can be 'blowing out' to clear the airway or part of relaxation during movement, usually accompanied by a lowered head and release of body tension.
- **Panic Snort**, which seems to be a rapid expelling of air when the horse gets a sudden fright. This snort is accompanied by a raised neck and tense body. It is instantly understood by other horses to indicate, "Look out for danger imminent".
- **Squeal**, which often accompanies a mare's intention to kick at a bothersome herd member. Sometimes related to breeding behavior.
- **Worry whinny** to link up with a friend out of view. This is usually a distress call that can vary in pitch and loudness in accordance with nature of the stress the horse is feeling.
- **Loud neigh** that carries great distances. It's often used when a whinny does not result in a response from the other horses or when returning home after an absence.
- **Scream** that accompanies rage, fear or pain.

Precise body language accompanies the horse's verbalizations, so in most cases the sounds amplify what the body language is saying. Sounds like the 'worry whinny' and 'loud neigh' are usually used communicate with a horse than is out of view.

22-2: Human Use of Verbal signals

A major problem with humans using verbal signals with their horses is that it is easy for people to suffer from 'verbal diarrhea'. We often talk so much that the sounds we make are meaningless to the horse. Our talking merely becomes background noise.

Good verbal signals for horses are:
- short
- distinct (and different from other verbal signals we intend to use)
- used with total consistency
- not surrounded by the 'noise' of general talking.

If we work with our horse silently, our mind can be more aware of the signals the horse is sending us moment to moment. Also, when we do use a verbal signal, it will be picked up more easily by the horse.

Verbal signals can be especially useful for:
- "whoa"
- "walk-on"
- upward transitions (in tune with body language, gesture and energy)
- downward transitions (in tune with body language, gesture and energy)
- turning right and left when long-reining
- backing up
- "load up" when asking to go into a trailer or through a narrow gate
- "lift" to lift a foot
- "ta" when finished with a foot and releasing it back to the ground
- "wait" when wanting the horse to stay parked (along with a gesture signal)
- a sharp "uh" as a conditioned inhibitor signal to arrest diving for grass or other unwanted behavior

- "yes", "good", "wahoo", or "excellent" as encouraging signals either to keep a movement going or at the end of a nice phase of movement along with the release (click&treat). For these, the horse might be tuning in more to the emotion being expressed, rather than the word itself, but it helps to use a consistent word.

23. Signal Type – Breathing and Energy

Our breath moving in and out is apparent to our horses because they are super aware of everything and because it relates closely to the energy we are expressing. Our energy level can be:
- relatively constant
- rising
- dropping
- turned down or turned away from the horse.

If we are careful and consistent, we can easily use our breath-in and breath-out as clear signals for the horse.

When we amplify our 'breath-in' it tells the horse that our energy is rising and we are preparing to ask for something.

If we amplify our 'breath-out', it turns into an audible sigh, which we can develop as a clear signal that our energy is coming down, and that we would like the horse's energy to come down as well.

This can become incredibly fine-tuned if the horse-person relationship is a close one. One of the challenges of a 10-obstacle Horse Agility course is to move smoothly between low energy obstacles, halts, and high energy obstacles.

When we are filming a Horse Agility course, I can easily lose a point by not raising or dropping my breath-controlled energy level at precisely the right moment.

The more we become aware of our breathing and how it communicates our energy to the horse, the more fun it is to use our breathing as a key signal to relate our intent.

24. Signal Type – Intent

You may have noticed scenes in natural history programs where zebra graze peacefully close to a pride of lions sleeping in the shade.

The zebra read the intent of the lions. They know what time of day the lions usually stir and hunt. They know, by reading the lions' body language, whether the lions have recently eaten or are getting ready to hunt.

Our horses have the same ability to read 'intent'. They easily pick up:

- when we are relaxed — in neutral, asking nothing
- when we are increasing our energy in preparation for sending a signal
- when we are in 'active neutral' during a task's execution
- when we are decreasing our energy.

Figure 22: Bridget is in 'neutral'. Boots understands this position as a signal to wait quietly with her head straight because she has been taught that a click&treat is only forthcoming when her head is facing forward.

In fact, many horses are more aware of these 'stages of being' than the handler. When we become more mindful about what our body is doing, it is easier for the horse to read our intention and our signal.

We can learn to be 'actively still' when not giving a signal.

Figure 23: Horse Agility task: I am in 'wait' mode while we wait 5 seconds halfway through a pair of rails. After the 'wait' I will ask her to back the rest of the way out of the rails.

When we are busy training, it's easy to move from one 'intent' to the next without remembering to stop frequently for 'dwell time' or 'soak time'. These pauses give us and the horse time to think about what we have just done.

During dwell time, the horse can be pleased that he made the right choice and earned release from the signal pressure (click&treat) for his efforts.

During dwell time, the handler can assess the quality of what just happened and if needed, adjust the plan according to the feedback from self and horse.

The more attention we can give to these 'pauses between the notes' of our activity, the easier it is to take stock of our own response and to consider how the horse has responded.

The more we build in pauses, the easier it is to remain in (or return to) our calm, centered core. And the easier it will be for the horse to remain in (or return to) his calm, centered core.

It is only from the calm, centered core that meaningful teaching and learning can proceed.

Horses Read Our Intent All the Time

If the horse (or the handler) gets into an emotional state, the first task is to return everyone to their calm, centered core. If a horse is flying around an enclosure or at the end of a line, we need to stay in our calm, centered core and withdraw our pressure (or click&treat) for the slightest sign of coming off the adrenalin.

At some point the horse will be able to recognize the withdrawal of our pressure or hear the click and retrieve the treat (either from our hand or tossed into a feed bucket).

Once he can engage with us, we soften our body language (click&treat) at every further sign that the horse is returning to calmness. Once he is calm, the horse will be able to re-engage his thinking mind. In other words, he will be able to switch from 'reactive' back to 'responsive'.

If the handler loses his calm, centered core and also becomes reactive, the horse will read the negative energy and not be helped by it. If that happens, it is wise to return the horse to his home and go away for a think and a hot beverage.

Horses are *always* linking the handler's behavior with possible consequences.

- Good signals achieve the intended behavior at low signal intensity.
- Bad signals don't achieve the intended behavior, no matter how intense we make them.
- Repeating or sustaining or amplifying a bad signal doesn't clarify anything for the horse. This is pointless nagging at best. At worst, it can cause confusion, anxiety or fear that will need a lot of careful unravelling.
- A good signal is clear, unequivocal and consistently used.
- To present clear signals, we must learn 'stillness' in our body and body extensions, when we are not giving a signal.

As mentioned earlier in Part 9, each signal has *intensity* and *duration*. When first teaching a new signal, we have to calibrate its intensity and duration so that it is effective. If our signal is not effective, then by definition, at that moment, it is not working as a signal for the behavior we want. Teaching a new signal also depends on *opportunity* and *timing*.

That means the right time of day and the right environment without undue distractions. It means applying the signal when the horse's body is in a position which allows it to carry out the request.

We have to reach the horse's mind first. Then the flexion, the weight shift, and the feet will follow the idea we have suggested to his mind. If we want the horse to be able to pick up his right front foot, we need to first ensure that his weight is over his left shoulder.

Since every horse, every handler and every horse-handler combination is different, only experimentation will lead to the best signal for each task we'd like our horse to do. The horse will often let us know which signal makes the most sense to him. We just have to learn to listen.

No matter how we try to put a gloss on it, our horse is captive to a foreign species whose language is foreign.

Fortunate horses have handlers who attempt to apply the following concepts to their training.

1. They emulate horse body language as much as a human can, thereby allowing the horse the dignity of his own language where possible. Learning basic horse body language allows a handler to communicate meaningfully with any horse. My book, *Learn Universal Horse Langue, No Ropes*, looks at this in detail.
2. They understand the individual horse's character type. More information about this is available in my book, *How to Create Good Horse Training Plans*. If you click 'home', the link is at the end of the first article.

3. They understand each horse's body language specifics (e.g. ears back can be a sign of concentration rather than bad thoughts, especially with mares).
4. They understand, as much as possible, the individual horse's previous experiences and how these may be impacting his present behavior.
5. They understand learning theory in terms of release reinforcement, reward reinforcement and inhibitors.
6. They understand how to use inhibitors when they are needed for the safety of the horse and/or the person.
7. They strive to give signals the correct *timing, intensity and duration* and apply them at the correct *opportunity*.

25 Signal Type - Environmental

Because they are so super-sensitive to everything in their environment, it doesn't take horses long to notice if we always do something at a certain spot or in a certain situation. We can use this to help teach patterns but we must be wary about setting a pattern into concrete in the horse's mind.

Many people will have experienced a rental trail horse who goes willingly to a certain point, but then turns for home, no matter what.

Environmental signals come in many forms.

- Safe fence-lines we can use to encourage straightness while teaching leading forward, backing up, lateral work. To be safe, the fence or gate is one that a horse's foot can't slip through.
- Ground rails or raised rails used to create lanes to make it easier for the horse to choose the option that we want.
- Objects and obstacles of many kinds to teach the horse boldness with new situations, e.g. tarps, barrels, water, big balls, pedestals, curtains, narrow gaps. Objects and obstacles are a superb way to initiate conversations with horses.

- Obstacles set up into weave patterns.
- A roomy space with a safe full-surround barrier to do gymnastic and cardio exercises without the need for a rope. Liberty play is fun.
- Rattling a feed bowl to call the horse in from the paddock.
- A saddle on a rail is an environmental signal to the horse. We would like him to move confidently to the saddle and 'greet it' by putting his nose on it.
- A halter or bridle is an environmental signal. We would like the horse to offer his head to go into it.
- A horse trailer is an environmental signal. We'd like the horse to see it as a comfort spot.
- A mounting block is an environmental signal. If we stand on it, we would like the horse to come over and offer us the opportunity to mount up.
- Nose targets and mats as foot targets are environmental signals we can use as 'rest spot' destinations.
- If we teach 'ground tying' by dropping the lead rope, this becomes an environmental signal
- Fresh grass is a huge environmental signal for a horse. Working on grass with confident, imaginative horses (who tend to be strongly food motivated) is always a challenge.
- A mat or a special spot can become an environmental signal if we use it consistently for the same purpose. For example, to make foot care easier on a sandy arena surface, I used an old double electric blanket for Boots to stand on. Before long, she knew, as soon as it came out, that it was foot care time.
- Trotting poles or jumps are environmental signals that tell the horse to prepare his energy and balance to navigate the obstacle (or avoid it).

Figure 24: Any obstacle to navigate is an environmental signal for the horse.

The 'Follow Factor'

Horses seem to have a natural tendency to follow anything moving away from them, and to move away from anything coming toward them.

If we are introducing something new to the horse, we can make it much easier by walking away with it first and allowing the horse to follow as far behind as he needs to feel safe.

With something like a wheelbarrow, bike, tractor, dragging rope, we need a helper to move in front of us with the object so we can follow along with the horse.

When I taught Boots about harness work, we went to harness club events and followed carts around. She learned about her cart by following it and checking it out. The 'follow factor' is the topic of Training Plan 3 in Part 33-7.

Figure 25: The Follow Factor: By walking away with a new object and letting the horse follow and put his nose on it when he feels confident enough, we are using his natural curiosity to build boldness with new things.

26. Signal Type - Marker Signal

A *marker signal* is also a 'sound' signal, but it has a significance totally different from any other sound or verbal signals we are using. It is the magical 'click' of Clicker Training.

A *marker signal* tells the horse that what he has just done is exactly what we want him to do. It is a special signal that tells the horse that a treat (something he especially values) will follow right away.

The click signals the horse to go into 'treat retrieval' mode, which usually means stopping if he was moving at the time of the click. The treat most highly valued by most horses is a small bit of food.

Treats often used include slices of carrot, apple or celery, horse pellets, grain, cereal, bits of dry bread, crackers, hay based pellets, popped popcorn, peppermints for a special effort, pumpkin seeds. Portions are tiny. It has to be something the horse really likes and looks forward to receiving.

The click (or whatever *marker signal* is being used) actually tells the horse these three things.

1. Yes, that's what I wanted.
2. You can stop now.
3. You can organize your body to get your treat out of my hand.

A: Treats with no Marker (Click-less Treats)

A well-mannered horse may be fine receiving an occasional hand-delivered treat without being requested to 'do something' for a click&treat.

However, if clicker training is going to become part of the education system, it is better to stay totally consistent. When approaching the horse, we can ask him to do a favorite move or a small task that we can reinforce with a click&treat.

Or if we are just checking on the horse we can put a treat into a feed bucket rather than feed it from our hand.

If I am going to visit my horse to check on her and say hello, I'll take a treat and ask her to back-up a couple of steps so I can click and offer the treat.

It is important to teach a clear signal to inform the horse when click&treat is finished for the moment. We need to have a way of letting the horse know that 'we are not playing right now' so we can move around with food in our pouch or pocket without getting ourselves into an unsafe situation.

My 'no more' signal consists of moving my arms horizontally in front of me, so they cross over each other a couple of times. This lets her know that no more treats will be forth- coming at this point in time.

Figure 26: This is my signal to let Boots know that we are finished with clicker training for the moment.

To me, it is essential that if I indicate 'finished', the horse appreciates that. Careful training ensures that the horse never feels free to demand a treat, even if he has offered a series of learned behaviors in the hope of getting his handler to click&treat.

If we don't ask for a behavior, there is no click. If there is no click, there will be no treat. This is basic foundation training if we want a safe and fun clicker savvy horse.

There is a great deal more information about Clicker Training in my book, *How to Begin Equine Clicker Training: Improving Horse-Human Communication.*

B: Treat-less Clicks

Some clicker trainers incorporate treat-less clicks into their work. To my mind, this complicates something that works perfectly well in its simple form.

They use clicks, **not** followed by treats, as a *'that's right but please keep going'* signal. It gives the horse the extra burden of having to work out when a click means, "Stop and get your treat," or when it means, "Keep going."

To work out when the click means 'stop for your treat', the horse obviously learns to observe other aspects of the handler's body language instead of being able to rely on the sound of the click.

For a 'please keep going' signal I find it much easier to use a special enthusiastic encouraging word such as 'Yes', 'Good', 'Wahoo' or 'Excellent'. The horse easily responds to the tone of voice as well as a consistently used word.

In my mind, treat-less clicks add a confusion that doesn't need to be present.

C: Awareness of what we are Clicking

Finding the *click point* we actually want can be tricky. We can click during the moment of activity, or we can click when a desired movement is finished.

This caused me a dilemma when I was teaching Smoky to jump at liberty. Did I click as he went into his arc over the jump, at the highest point of his jump or after he had landed?

The first time I decided to click as he was jumping. Because Smoky is so highly food-motivated, he basically stopped his jump in mid-air to get himself into treat-retrieval mode as fast as he could. A bit more thought on my part was obviously needed.

Eventually it turned out that just at landing was a good place to click for this particular horse.

Another example to illustrate the importance of the exact timing of our click arose when I taught Boots to ring a bell for five seconds (another Horse Agility challenge).

I used a cowbell suspended on a string. She rings it by nuzzling it with her lips. Since she is clicker savvy and confident with nose targets, my training plan was to click&treat for:

1. touching her nose to the bell
2. touching it strongly enough to make it ring
3. nuzzling it to make it ring twice in a row

4. nuzzling it to make it ring three times in a row
5. nuzzling it to make it ring four times in a row
6. nuzzling it to make it ring five times in a row.

Straightforward enough, you say. So I thought when I started. However, to get her to keep on nuzzling the bell, I had to be super careful, after slice 2, to click while she was still actively engaged in nuzzling, not when she took her nose off the bell (i.e. when she finished a ringing episode).

I wanted more of the nuzzling, not the 'finish'. She would stop and look to me saying, "I'm finished, where is my click&treat?" I had to rev up my observation and clicker timing skills to click the moments she was still doing the ringing.

A short video clip called *"Free-Shaping Ringing a Bell"* in my *Free-Shaping* playlist shows us playing with this task. It pays to carefully consider when we are sounding the click and what message the horse is receiving. Is it the message we think we are sending?

D: Phasing out Click&Treat

As part of Clicker Training, a horse needs to be aware that known behaviors we ask for will sometimes result in click&treat and sometimes not. For things the horse knows well, simple release reinforcement lets him know he was right. It's important that basic daily handling and husbandry can be done without using click&treat when the occasion arises.

If we don't educate the horse to that level, we are short-changing his intelligence and setting up future situations that can be problematic for us and the horse.

The first language every horse already knows is release reinforcement. We apply signal pressure and remove it the instant the horse complies.

We do him a dis-service if we don't learn Universal Horse Language and use it to teach the horse appropriate responses to the unusual pressures put on him in the human-centric world he is forced to live in.

Ropes, small pens, halters, trailers and all the other paraphernalia we use are totally foreign to a horse's natural life. Why would any horse with common sense jump over an object when it is only a step or two to walk around it?

Signal pressure and 'release' of that pressure is what horses innately understand. It's the main element of horse-horse communication between herd members. They don't have any trouble understanding each other.

When someone asks us to do something, we can feel the 'signal pressure' they are putting on us. When we complete the task, that pressure is gone. Most of the world works that way.

Horses are not blank slates on which we write what we want. They are complex beings whose evolutionary history is as long as the human one. They have a language, a natural group dynamic and etiquette about how to behave within the group.

When someone at home or at work asks us to do something, we feel the 'signal pressure' of their request. The only way to make the pressure go away is to do the task or say, "No." When we put on our work clothes or a work uniform, we feel the signal pressure of what our job expects from us.

There's no reason to think that horses don't feel signal pressure in a similar way. When he is outfitted in his halter and rope or riding/driving gear, or playing at liberty in an enclosed area, the well-educated horse understands what is happening and willingly responds with behaviors we have carefully taught.

The less educated horse will say, "No," more often because he does not understand what is being asked of him.

Working for a reward, rather than only for a release of signal pressure, is strongly motivating for horses, just as it is for all of us. Receiving the treat motivates the horse to repeat what he did in order to earn the 'click&treat' again.

All animal actions are geared toward *identity* (with group or place), *security* (of food and shelter) and *stimulation*. Horses living in the wild lead a life full of all sorts of stimulation. Mostly these deal with:

- awareness of predators
- running from real or perceived danger
- deciding if a danger is indeed real or not
- curious inspection of anything unusual
- dealing with seasonal change; extreme cold or dry and the food/water challenges that accompany these
- breeding
- giving birth and raising/protecting foals
- within-group relationships to sort/maintain the social order
- mutual grooming
- continuous movement during grazing and browsing
- moving between grazing areas and water supply
- marking and inspecting home range boundaries
- keeping tabs on neighboring horse groups
- dealing with death via predation or injury
- dealing with the rearrangement of the social order if a group member dies or leaves, or a new member joins the group
- stallions initiating a challenge or defending a challenge.

Natural horse life is a veritable soap opera of challenges and stimulation. It's hard for us to provide the same level of stimulation for our captive horses. The lucky ones spend their non-human time with other horses, moving freely 24/7 in large fields or on a track system and are part of a group culture of some sort.

Teaching our horse useful and fun things with click&treat reward reinforcement is one way to add stimulation to a life that may otherwise be exceedingly boring and physiologically unhealthy.

27. Signal Type - Feel

Feel is an aspect of horsemanship that sometimes seems elusive, but it doesn't have to be. It is closely linked with the idea of empathy. Empathy itself is the ability to 'feel' what another being is probably feeling.

When dealing with horses, empathy and feel are involved with everything we do. The more we understand about the nature of horses as a prey species that depends on group life for security, the more empathetic we can be when our horse shows us that he is uncomfortable about something we are asking him to do.

The more we understand that the horse's digestive system is geared toward a steady flow of low nutrient forage, the better job we can do at providing such forage. We know that to keep the horse comfortable, we must feed the bacteria in the gut in a way that keeps them happy.

Horses have small stomachs and a large caecum where bacteria break down the food so it can be absorbed by the horse. These bacteria need a constant flow of food and do not like sudden changes of diet.

The more we understand how the horse's circulation system depends on slow, regular walking movement over 24 hours, the less inclined we will be to confine horses in boxes. After all, they are not chocolates.

The horse's feet compress and expand with each step the horse takes. Foot movements work like four extra pumps to help send blood the very long way up the legs back to the heart.

Horses step along as they graze. The only time they are still is for the few hours that they sleep, which are spread over 24 hours. Consistent movement is an integral part of horse circulation health.

Horses are naturally active on a 24-hour rhythm, not a day/night rhythm like we are. By 'putting them in at night' and by 'feeding them meals' in one place, we are seriously mucking about with their movement, their blood circulation and their natural biorhythms.

Many horse problems stem from unnatural housing and unnatural feeding regimes as well as the damage caused by nailing inflexible steel shoes to a dynamic live foot mechanism.

As we develop empathy and 'feel' about what a horse is experiencing in the strange human-based world in which he finds himself, it becomes easier to know what we should do to ensure the horse is as comfortable as possible.

A horse high on adrenalin will find comfort in being allowed to trot or run the adrenalin out of his system. When he becomes high-headed and agitated, a handler with feel gives him the opportunity to move until he can switch from reactive mode to responsive mode.

A strong-spirited, low-energy horse can be extremely frustrating. A handler with feel for this sort of horse will use motivation as much as possible, and appreciate the reliable nature of this type of horse once he is on-side with the handler rather than trying to outwit his handler.

As soon as we can see our horse, he can see us. As soon as he can see us, he is gauging our energy level. He is 'feeling' us. A person with 'feel' will be doing the same with the horse – gauging his mood, the way he is moving or grazing, checking for anything out of the ordinary.

When a handler develops 'feel' of this sort, he is not frustrated by undesirable horse behaviors. He seeks their cause and adjusts his Individual Education Program (IEP) to accommodate the horse. This is the essence of a handler's emotional neutrality.

Horses don't do things just to annoy us. At any moment in time the horse is doing what he believes is the best thing do.

With careful education, we can enlarge the horse's comfort zone and areas of expertise. We can expand his repertoire of things he can do with confidence.

It takes considerable time and effort, but done at the horse's pace, he will gain skills to help him through his whole life.

27-1: Some concepts of 'feel'

'Feel' comes in many guises. Here are some of them.

1. Feeling the difference between reaction and response
2. Realizing that every horse will feel different, and that to the horse, each handler feels different
3. Knowing the precise moment to release signal pressure (click&treat)
4. Acknowledging the difference between teaching and forcing
5. Knowing when we are pushing too much, resulting in a loss of willingness
6. Knowing when we are pausing too much, resulting in a loss of interest
7. Knowing when we are petting too much, resulting in a loss of position in the group
8. Recognizing physical well-being, so that lack of wellness stands out
9. Finding the 'balance' between the two extremes of 'unbalanced'
10. Able to cause a subtle shift in the horse so he regains balance
11. Staying grounded when the horse loses his physical, mental and/or emotional balance
12. Ability to 'wait' for lesson absorption or for a shift in balance
13. Ability to ignore unwanted behavior and quietly 're-set' a task
14. Understanding a specific horse's underlying character type
15. Recognizing when the horse is ready to learn something new
16. Recognizing when the horse is ready to move on to the next slice of the new learning

17. Recognizing when the horse-human connection is present and when it is absent
18. Not taking the horse's trust for granted
19. Understanding the lives of horses in the wild; their natural 24 hour and seasonal rhythms
20. Understanding physical, mental and emotional thresholds of a particular horse
21. Understanding how habituation works
22. Understanding how desensitization works
23. Understanding how sensitization works
24. Physical feel through the rope
25. Physical feel through the reins
26. Physical and emotional feel through the whole body when riding
27. Feel for two-way communication playing at Liberty. If the horse decides to leave, knowing how to motivate him to join up again or deciding to call it a day
28. Knowing when to stop a lesson, or a part within the lesson
29. Understanding that the way the handler feels is instantly picked up by the horse, good feelings and bad feelings equally

Habituation

Habituation comes about by exposing a horse to a situation often enough (using approach and retreat at first to gain confidence) so that it becomes an accepted part of his life. For example, lots of short trailer rides that start at home and end at home.

Desensitization and Sensitization

Desensitization is taking a horse through a learning process so he knows that a specific thing or place is not a threat to his safety. It includes helping your horse get bolder in all kinds of situations and with all kinds of obstacles.

There are things to which we want our horse to be desensitized and things to which we want him to be sensitized.

We want him to be sensitive to our position in the relationship and to our signals when we are doing ground games or riding.

We want him desensitized to the discomfort of a saddle and girth but sensitive to our position in the saddle, our signals for 'go' and 'whoa', change of direction, disengagement, backing up, and maybe eventually, the more sophisticated moves of competitive horse sports.

The best way to ruin sensitivity is through nagging. When we strive to do things that build rapport with our horse, we are also building sensitivity. Generally, our horse's sensitivity will reflect our own sensitivity and consistency.

The best way to sensitize our horse is to begin each signal with the least intensity possible, then increase the intensity to just as much as we need to gain the response. This is what 'horse whispering' is all about.

A bit more about Feel with the Rope during Ground Work

With practice and experience, our gross motor skills around rope handling gradually turn into finesse rope handling skills.

In the same way, a horse may initially need an amplified rope signal to elicit the behavior we want, but as he comes to understand the request, he will be able to respond with more and more finesse.

It is important that as the horse responds with more accuracy and finesse, we lighten the intensity of our signals as quickly as possible. The horse can only become as light as our signals are light.

Figure 27: Note the lightness of Lorraine's touch on the rope as she asks Bob to follow the feel of the rope to step over the rail.

27-2: Large Signal Dilemma

It's important that we don't get stuck in the *large signal dilemma*. Sometimes people find a large signal that works and habitually use it forever to shout at the horse. They never think to develop a small whisper of a signal to give the same message.

Such handlers can help their horses by focusing on developing feel. Every horse will feel different.

Once we activate rope signal pressure, feel comes into play, allowing us to release the pressure the instant the horse softens to the pressure.

We close our hands or fingers slowly to give the horse time to feel the pressure coming, then we open our hands quickly the moment we can feel him responding to our pressure.

This release of pressure is the only way horses have of knowing what it is we want them to do. If we also use Clicker Training, the click is simultaneous with the release and the treat is offered immediately (ideally within one second).

If we release (or click) at the wrong time, the horse will not understand what we want.

Feel is inseparable from good timing. We have to be able to feel the moment we should release. The video clip called *Thin-slice Soft Yield to Rein Signals* from my *Thin Slicing Examples* playlist gives a good demonstration, especially from time mark 4:50, of how easily bad timing can confuse a horse.

If our feel for the timing of the release is faulty, we are dropping the horse into a cauldron of confusion. Some horses will try to fill in as best they can.

Others may shut down and stop trying. Others will become energized with anxiety and want to move their feet to get away from a situation they don't understand.

A handler with a good sense of feel will know which of the above is happening, and adjust his training to bring the horse back to a place of confidence to try again, which might be on another day.

When horses put pressure on each other, the pressure goes off as soon as the other horse moves away. In the wild there are no ropes or artificial barriers that stop the horse from moving away. He gets instant release reinforcement. That is what good trainers seek to emulate. Timing and feel are totally inter-related.

When we do ground work, we are 'holding hands' via the rope. Alongside the rope signals, the horse is noticing our body orientation, our body language, our gestures and maybe our touch to help him work out what we want.

That all changes as soon as the handler mounts up.

A bit more about Feel through the Reins

As mentioned earlier, when we ride we suddenly disappear from the horse's field of vision. As well as being out of sight, we expect the horse to have his nose 'out in front'. For some horses this is a big ask if their previous experience is limited to the comfort of following the handler's lead on the ground.

Before my horse was started under saddle, I spent a lot of time walking on the road with her, keeping myself positioned beside the saddle where I would be when riding.

This way, she gained confidence about having her nose out in front as we moved along together. *#26-#30* and *#41-#46* inclusive *HorseGym with Boots* playlist look at these leading positions which are also detailed in my book, *Walking with Horses*.

It also helps if the horse understands long-reining and has gone through the Universal Horse Language program so he already understands 'guiding from behind' in several contexts.

Figure 28: Teaching rein signals with long-reining can give the horse a big head start when it comes to being ridden.

Essentially, when we are riding, the horse must learn a revamped language. Where he could respond to our visual body language signals he now has to receive directional and transition information via the reins and the rider's body tension and weight shifts.

It is easy to see how a horse with an experienced, balanced, soft-handed rider, who has taught verbal and touch signals on the ground, will get a much better deal than a novice horse struggling with a novice unbalanced rider unfamiliar with ground work.

Some horses know a lot of riding signals but not much else because they have not been educated with ground work. Some people feel safer riding their horse than being on the ground with him.

This is sad, because both the horse and the handler are missing out on fun and the rider-less gymnastic exercises that benefit the horse.

It's sad because it sometimes results in riding horses that are unreliable and dangerous to handle for everyday management, through no fault of their own.

Feel and the Ridden Horse

As mentioned earlier, the horse's natural balance is hugely compromised when a rider climbs aboard. It takes time and opportunity for him to re-calibrate his balance with the rider at each gait.

The horse needs to build up his confidence as well as develop his muscles to cope with the unusual loading.

The old masters allowed a long time to achieve this. This is not always the case nowadays when time is money. Young horses with promise are commonly exploited for human competitions before they have matured enough to endure the pressure more easily.

Feel and the Rider

A rider with feel unconsciously moves his body in rhythm with the horse's body. One way to help develop this sort of feel is to ask the horse to move forward in a safe, enclosed area without attempting to direct where the horse goes (Parelli 'passenger lesson'). The rider can focus exclusively on the feel of the horse and learn to relax into the movement rather than tense up against it.

The same exercise allows the horse time to get the feel of that particular rider, so it can suit both parties.

However, that Parelli exercise might not be suitable for every horse or every rider. Safety must be considered first. In some cases, it is safer to have the novice rider come along as a 'passenger' while a handler on the ground asks the horse to:

- initiate the halt-walk transition
- go for a relaxed walk between destination points
- initiate the walk-halt transition
- initiate the halt-back up transition
- initiate the walk-trot transition
- walk in a circle on a long line
- weave a series of obstacles
- step over obstacles
- move between obstacles
- move around obstacles
- initiate trot-canter transition on long line
- initiate canter-trot transition on long line
- long-rein between destinations.

As the novice rider develops a feel for the way the horse moves, responsibility for the signals can gradually transfer to the rider.

To begin with, the rider does best without using the reins, so his or her focus can be totally on how everything feels. It's good if the rider can close his eyes and tell the ground handler what the horse is doing.

I had an interesting experience when I was teaching such a passenger lesson. The rider was willing to close her eyes. I asked her to tell me when the horse did something that felt different. I led the horse along and gently asked it to move smoothly from walk to halt and into back-up. The rider had no idea that the horse was backing up rather than walking forward.

Even if we have ridden for a long time, this exercise can be fun. It may highlight places where we can improve our feel.

Natural horsemanship has done many horses a big favor by getting riders out of their horses' mouths until their feel and balance have reached a level of competence.

Many people then go on to enjoy bridle-less riding, demonstrating that a tuned-in horse easily feels the balance shifts and touches that have become the signals for their secret riding language.

Many horses with a history of mouth pain from bits become totally different when ridden bit-less. Pain from bits can be linked to so many of a horse's life experiences that it can color their whole relationship with humans.

Horse mouth autopsies have identified the copious damage people do to horses by putting pressure on hard metal in the most sensitive part of the horse anatomy.

When riding for pleasure, although we have on a bridle, a halter with reins, or side-pull head gear, we can always ride 'bridle-less' by refining our other signals and using the head gear touch only if necessary for clarity.

Everything we do with a horse is about asking him to move his feet in a particular way. Whether we want him to stand still, gallop, climb up on a pedestal or lift his foot so we can clean it out, we are wanting to direct his feet.

The most important aspect of riding, once we can relax into the feel of the horse's movement subconsciously, is to learn the feel of the horse's footfall in the various gaits.

We can focus on footfall watching video footage slowed down to get a picture of how the feet move at each gait. Then the challenge is to learn to feel the horse's footfall while riding, without looking down.

We need to be able to feel when a hind leg is coming forward under our seat and when a front foot lifts off the ground.

Some people find this much easier than others. With a good Individual Education Program *written for ourselves*, divided into small slices (addressing one foot at a time) and not expecting too much all at once, we can all learn to feel footfall.

Actually, it is not 'footfall' we need to feel, as much as 'foot-rise'. It is at the moment the foot is *rising* that we can influence where it goes next.

28. Signal Type - Context:

Context might be best explained with a series of examples. In some ways, context can be a subset of environmental signals.

Example 1: Time of day routines

If we have established routines for the day to day care of a horse, he will read the context of the routines when he sees us at certain times. For example, during some seasons I go out early first thing to give my horse hay. My presence at that time is not a signal that we will be doing anything else.

After I clean the paddocks, it is our routine to go for a road walk. After our walk and any *HorseGym* we are doing that morning, we return to the yard.

We generally clean feet at this point, so Boots lines herself up in the shelter and waits for me to get my gear. She may still have her halter and lead on, or she may be at liberty. The gate out of the yard is open.

After foot care, we have an 'end of session' routine of games with click&treat. Only when these are finished and I show her that I have no more treats, does she wander off.

I return to the yard at dusk to feed and she will be waiting. Like all of us, routine gives a sense of security and an ability to look forward to what usually happens next.

It's good to have some flexibility built into a routine, so things happen at a general time of day, not specifically 'on the dot', because some horses (and people) will then stress about something being later than usual.

Most horses show specific behaviors in the context of the timing of their everyday care. In the wild or on the range, horses have a 24-hour rhythm of resting and activity.

Example 2: Gate Safety

Because I strip graze, with a new strip of grass once or twice a day, my horse understandably looks forward to the gate opening so she can speed off down the track to the new grass. To avoid being trampled due to her excitement, we had to develop a careful Individual Education Program that allowed me to open the gate safely.

Our program required that Boots learned to wait politely while I open the gate. Then I ask her to take two or three steps backwards to earn a click&treat. That allows me time to move aside and give an arm gesture to release her through the gate.

I taught the stages at liberty, but it could be taught first with halter and lead rope on. One would then have to add in polite un-haltering, followed by a step back, click&treat, allowing the handler time to step aside. Some horses will leap into a canter from the halt.

To break the habit of bolting through the gate before it was properly open, I used a long body extension and insisted, with as much energy as I needed, that the space of the open gate belonged to me until I moved away from it.

The click&treat dynamic worked well because I was able to ask her to do something specific; in this case to step back several steps, in order to earn the reward.

For the first week or so, I needed to be very firm. For a few weeks after that, I made sure to always carry a body extension just in case I needed to make myself larger.

Gradually I noted that she knew exactly how far the gate swung inwards, and she would stand and wait beyond that spot, back up as soon as I turned toward her, and accept her treat after I clicked, before departing for the grass.

Recently we transferred the behavior to a different gate with little fuss. Boots and I now have a protocol of specific behaviors in the context of a gate onto fresh grass.

Example 3: Food bucket delivery

I use the same principle when delivering a bucket of feed. It's normal for a horse to be keen to get at his special ration in a bucket. It's another situation where a horse, unaware of his size and strength, can inadvertently injure a person.

To avoid being stepped on or head-butted, I now always ask for three steps back, which gives me time to put the bucket into its holder. Then I click and the food in the bucket is the reward reinforcement.

We do this totally consistently, so seeing me walking across the yard with her dinner bucket has become a context for Boots to come with me politely, then dance a few steps backwards while I place the bucket, click, and move away.

Example 4: Handler Position

Each of the Eight Leading Positions (see *#26 HorseGym with Boots*) is a new context because each one has a different handler position.

As noted earlier, the handler's body orientation is a major part of a signal during ground work. The Eight Leading Positions are:

1. Straight in front, facing same direction as horse; horse stays directly behind in single file
2. In front but off to one side, facing same direction as horse; horse's nose stays behind our shoulder
3. Beside the horse's head, neck, or shoulder, facing forward
4. Behind the withers (alongside ribs/saddle position), facing forward
5. Beside the butt, facing forward
6. Behind horse, facing forward
7. In front, facing horse
8. Facing the horse's shoulder, ribs or hindquarters.

Let's look specifically at the context of being in Leading Position Six, behind the horse. We can teach this as a guiding position by walking quietly behind the horse after we have asked him to move off, on request, from one hay pile to another pile of hay. (See #77 *HorseGym with Boots*.)

If we have set up several hay piles, we can ask the horse to move off one pile, then step in behind him as he walks to another. This is part of the *Learn Universal Horse Language* program.

Later we can use this same context when we teach the horse about long-reining, or asking him to load up into a trailer while we stay behind at the ramp.

We can teach long-reining long before the horse is old enough to ride. It gives him a chance to learn all about signals from behind the drive line.

Riding is merely an extension of 'guiding from behind' at the walk. We are guiding the horse from behind his drive line (everything behind his withers).

If he already understands the context of being asked to do things from behind, it will be much easier for him to understand what you want when you first mount up.

Getting the horse comfortable with us 'guiding him from behind' at liberty between piles of hay, then teaching him long-reining consolidated with soft rein signals, gives him a huge advantage when we suddenly want to manage his feet by sitting on him.

The main context of 'being behind him' stays the same. Only the specifics of the situation have changed. (See Training Plan 8, Part 33-12, *Light Rope/Rein Response*.)

The horse has a much better chance of keeping his mental and emotional confidence intact when we work like this, in small stages or 'slices' toward the outcome that we want.

Each of the other Leading Positions is a context for the horse when we do ground work. For example, Leading Position One (straight in front, facing away) resembles horses moving along in single file heading to new grazing or following a track to a water source.

Boots and I often use it on our morning walks when we are just moseying along, enjoying the scenery and the fresh air. She relaxes into an elongated walk.

The specifics for the context of 'please walk behind me' can change. I may need her to walk behind me along a narrow track, between cars or trot behind me through a narrow Horse Agility obstacle.

Handler body position and orientation can become integral parts of our signals. Horse Agility requires a loose lead rope at all times, with a point docked each time it goes tight.

Figure 29: Turning my shoulders and hips is the signal Boots reads to turn with me. No halter touch signals via the rope are needed. In Horse Agility, each tight rope loses one point.

Once I started delving into the detail of the Eight Leading Positions, it became apparent that it was the topic of a whole book of Training Plans and a whole series of video clips.

The clips are #39-#64, inclusive, in my *HorseGym with Boots* playlist.

Example 5: Destinations

Like the rest of us, horses are most comfortable if they know their destination. Taking a horse on a new ride is usually more fraught with emotion than going out on a familiar route. It is the same as our apprehension during our first drive in an unknown area.

We can build destinations into our horse's Education Program. If we teach our horse to anticipate a reward (relaxation and/or click&treat) at nose targets (cloths or plastic bottles hung around) or at foot targets (mats on the ground), we can use these for motivation.

We are giving the horse a reason to move with us from A to B. (See *#3-#15* inclusive *HorseGym with Boots*.)

With destination targets tied or laid out around our work area or along a track, the horse soon willingly seeks them out and our training can focus on different things to do on our way to the next destination. Knowing that there will be a destination with a rest and/or click&treat, is highly motivating for horses, just as it is for us. When was the last time you left home without knowing your destination?

If we work without destinations, it is hard for the horse to have a sense of accomplishment. He is on a continuous mystery tour, expected to do what he is told, much as if he were a bicycle or a motorbike.

When we first ask a horse to walk out or ride out away from home, we can set up destination points before we leave. As the horse becomes familiar with the route, the targets can be further and further apart and eventually be phased out.

Systematic training like this allows the horse to gradually gain confidence about going away from home. We learn to see and listen for the edges of the horse's comfort zone. Once that is established, we can ask for a bit more, *but not so much that we burst his bubble of confidence.*

Once walking or riding out is a relaxed experience, we can rely on handy environmental destinations, like a stump, big rock, or the corners of a paddock, for a rest. We can find special grazing spots, a shady tree, or water to splash in. The horse will happily accept these as new destinations.

Destination points are exceedingly helpful contexts to the gradual development of a horse's willingness to follow our suggestions.

Example 6: Position of an Object

Horses living a natural life are highly tuned in to the position of objects in their surroundings. They notice the slightest change. They are also curious. Their curiosity causes them to investigate the unfamiliar to see if it is harmless, or not.

It is for this reason that I make sure that my horse is present when I set up a new Agility Course. It can take longer while she stands on the tarp I am trying to unfold, pushes through the pool noodles while I am trying to insert ten of them into their holders, or walks through the curtain and waits for me to notice.

But it means she is building a picture in her mind about where each object or obstacle is placed. When it is something new or unusual, like a tunnel, she has free time to investigate.

When I had a mounting platform in the arena, I used it to get on and off. Boots also used it to suggest to me when she'd had enough and maybe it was time to get off and do something else. The context of the platform was firmly in her mind.

If we usually put our trailer or truck in the same spot for loading our horse, that position of the vehicle will become a context for the horse to look forward to loading up, or to worry if he is anxious about traveling.

I have a little stool I sit on beside my horse's shoulder for trimming front feet. I use the same stool placed in front of her to signal tummy tucks. Sitting down low while doing the tummy tucks encourages her to flex at the poll as well as rock back.

The position of the stool gives her a context for what we are about to do. Beside her shoulder, we are trimming a foot. Directly in front of her, we are doing tummy tucks. At other times, I may take the stool into paddock to just sit and share time and space on a sunny day.

Example 7: Arena Markers

I used to think that if I taught my horse to pick up cones or rags, I wouldn't be able to use the cones or rags as pattern markers. I was wrong.

When I set out cones or rags, I expect my horse to approach one and pick it up because we have had many lessons on picking things up. She does that, but if no click&treat is forthcoming for the 'picking up', she willingly changes to work with the movement pattern I've set up with the markers.

At the end of the session, we go around together and she picks up the cones or rags so we can put them away.

Horses appear to have a good understanding of context.

Example 8: Round Pen Contexts

What we do the first time we take the horse into a round pen will set the round pen context for the horse.

Context One:

We can furnish the round pen with several piles of hay, a chair and a book to read. Our plan is to lead the horse to the pen, take off his halter, sit in our chair and read our book. Our intention is to spend time and space with the horse in a safe, contained area. The horse might choose the hay or he might choose to snooze beside the handler's chair or as far from the handler as possible.

When the horse is relaxed spending quiet time with us in the round pen, we can ask him to move away from the pile of hay he is enjoying to go find another one. We move our chair to sit by our claimed pile. Our behavior resembles that of another horse.

After a while, we may decide that the pile the horse is now eating looks better, so we quietly ask him to move away and claim it with our chair, followed by reading some more of our book.

Context Two:

Another way people use round pens is chase the horse around the perimeter until he gets so tired or anxious that he begins to look toward the handler in the middle, at which point the handler releases the driving pressure.

After a while, most horses realize that moving toward the handler and 'joining up' with him is the quickest way to get the driving pressure to stop.

Context Three:

If we introduce the space of the round pen with Context One above, we can move on to add objects and obstacles that help us teach the horse the appropriate responses to pressure he needs to get along in his human-based environment without trauma.

We can use the edge of the round pen as a boundary to teach transitions and gait maintenance without the interference of ropes. Working without a rope allows us to refine our body language and gesture signals as well as being clearer with our energy and our intent.

It is easy to see how the context of the round pen in the horse's mind will depend on how he is introduced to it and what he is asked to do when he visits it.

Example 9: Shows and Events

Before we depart for a show or an event, we have hopefully built the horse's confidence with the context of loading up and traveling. There is a Training Plan for this in my book, *Natural Horsemanship Study Guide*, as well as one of my DVD and Notes sets, both of which are listed in the *Further Resources Available* at the end of the book.

Ideally, we take the horse to shows/events where we are not taking part so we can spend all our time with the horse as he gets used to the noise, smells and general anxiety given off by many of the other horses.

If we can take him with a confident, seasoned horse that he knows, the new horse will carefully observe and emulate the seasoned horse.

The same is true for walking out or riding out away from home, confidence with water, reaction to bicycles, bridges, dogs or children. There is more about this in Part 29 about modelling behavior.

Habituation versus Flooding

Taking the horse to a series of events just to hang out is the ideal way to habituate him to the context of horse events away from home. Habituation is gradually getting used to something by regular exposure.

Habituation allows the horse time to adjust and keeps his dignity intact. It allows him to maintain emotional control.

If, on the other hand, we enter a show or book into a clinic, take the horse along and expect him to travel, get used to everything at the venue plus perform all on the same day, we are 'flooding' the horse's coping system.

Usually this results in a desire to escape the situation. Since that is usually not possible due to ropes, reins or small spaces, the horse's only other choice is to 'shut down'.

'Flooding' has worked to inure horses to the horrors of war, but if we don't want a horse that is emotionally and mentally shut down, gradual habituation is a far better way to reach our goal.

29. Horses Learn via Observation and Modelling

Sometimes Boots and I work at liberty through a set pattern of obstacles for a Horse Agility competition. Boots picks up the pattern quickly and likes to 'get it right'.

Other times, we do liberty free play among the obstacles where she can earn a click&treat for following my suggestion of the moment. I model the direction and energy levels, Boots follows my suggestions.

Figure 30: Boots is imitating my leg movement as we play stretching games.

When horses can watch another horse's training session, they often seem to absorb some of the learning. Sometimes I teach one horse something new while a second horse is watching. When the second horse has his turn to learn the same thing he already seems to understand a large part of the lesson.

This is not astounding. Horses living natural lives can only learn by watching other horses and copying the behaviors modeled by them. It starts as soon as a foal is on its feet. The urge to find the teats and suckle is instinctive, but after that, the foal learns what to avoid and what is safe, by noting the behavior of his mother and other herd members.

It explains why horses reared in very un-natural situations often have no idea about horse herd etiquette. They have not been in a multi-age horse group to learn acceptable group behavior.

If they are kept in small spaces, they have no chance to develop physical balance through continuous movement on uneven terrain.

If they are raised in isolation without a stimulating environment, they will not have the mental skills to cope adequately with changes in the future.

If they are physically constrained and mentally unstimulated, their emotional health as well as their physiological well-being, will suffer. Keeping horses in small spaces is far from the lifestyle for which they are genetically programmed.

Such horses have nowhere to move, nothing to observe, and are often fraught with internal health problems due to poor circulation and unnatural feeding regimes.

It is not surprising that emotional problems, related to fear and anxiety, arise when people put gear on them and expect them to behave in a certain way.

Foals introduced at birth to friendly humans will tend to consider humans as part of their extended herd. This is called 'imprinting'.

Properly done, it allows the foal to form a positive picture of humans as friendly, natural beings present in their environment.

Figure 31: Having fun with obstacles & objects enrichens a captive horse's life.

Young horses introduced to objects and obstacles in a fun way will grow up with more confidence in the human-centric world.

An enriched environment builds confidence with new experiences. It also engages the thinking part of the brain, so building more neural pathways.

Horses love to play and they are innately curious. The more we can develop these features of horses, the more enjoyment we can have, and the more bearable we can make the horse's un-natural life.

30. How Horses Converse with Us

30-1: Why Would a Horse Befriend a Human?

It's interesting that the larger animals people have domesticated, except for cats and rabbits, are all group-living animals. Group-living animals have a carefully evolved social order.

This social order meets the needs of the species by balancing the benefits of living together with the competitive tensions that result because all members of the group require the same resources. Each species has its own rules of social engagement.

The social order or group hierarchy (sometimes called the 'pecking order') allows the group members to live together without constant individual jockeying for the best food, water, shade, shelter.

When times are good, there is plenty for everyone. When drought or cold make resources scarce, the social order ensures that the more dominant (or in some cases the more fortunate) members get the best of the limited resources and therefore have a greater chance at passing on their genetic material to the next generation. This is the basic reality of life in the wild.

By insinuating themselves into the existing social order of herd animals, people have domesticated cattle, sheep, goats, pigs, horses, dogs, geese, chickens, turkeys, elephants, camels, alpaca and llama.

People often think that they have brought the animal into their social order. The animal, however, sees us as part of his social order. It is by infiltrating the animal's social order, that we become accepted by the animal as 'one of us'.

To successfully communicate with a particular species, we need to learn, appreciate and use the social etiquette of that species. When the animals accept us without fear, we have become an honorary member of their group.

As long as we have a working knowledge of the species' social etiquette and stick with it, animals seem very forgiving of our funny shape and very bad accents when we speak their language.

Horses are especially tolerant of our shortcomings. It is not hard to learn and use Universal Horse Language as outlined in my book, *Learn Universal Horse Language: No Ropes.*

If horses could scream like pigs, there would be a lot of screaming going on at places like horse events and 'horse training' facilities. The sheer size, power and quickness of horses understandably makes people fearful.

Fearful people tend to grasp, hold, confine and use force to get their way. That has been the fate of most horses for many, centuries while they were the transport of human commerce and war.

Slowly, in societies no longer dependent on horsepower, people are coming to recognize that conversations with horses (donkeys and mules) can be:

- subtle
- entered into without coercion
- spoken in a way that allows mutual understanding
- organized with reward reinforcement as well as release reinforcement.

Let's look at the ways a horse is able to communicate with us. As we become more aware, we will start to listen and 'hear' more and more.

30-2: Signals Horses Use to Speak to Us

A: Signs of anxiety or fear-based stress

- Whole body tension
- High head
- Staring eyes
- Stiff ears
- Tight lips
- Tightly clamped tail — j-shaped tail if fear is extreme
- Desire to move feet away from the situation is always a first response and why people use ropes and small pens
- The dropped head of a horse that has gone 'internal' – a sort of non-blinking paralysis called catalepsy

B: Signs of a horse releasing tension

- Sighing
- Chewing/licking (not related to food)
- Yawning
- Shaking head/neck (not related to flies)
- Blowing out
- Extreme blinking
- Able to respond to a light signal

C: Signs of a horse in a state of mental, emotional and physical relaxation

- Soft, relaxed tail (will lift tail if we gently rub under it)
- Floppy ear tips
- Soft eyes
- Lowered head (poll level with the withers)
- Relaxed, loose or floppy bottom lip

- Soft body outline
- Relaxed cocked hip
- Curiosity with a soft aspect
- If in motion, a soft outline; poll level with withers and rhythmic movement
- Happy to stay in our presence

D: Signs of a horse expressing annoyance or responding to pain
- Swishing tail (in a continuum from a quick flick to full-fledged tail-wringing)
- Ears pinned (which is different from ears just 'back')
- Snaking of neck toward the cause of annoyance (another horse, dog, person)
- Turning butt toward the annoyance as a warning that a kick could follow
- If wearing a bit, gaping mouth, constant mouthing trying to adjust the bit's position to be less painful, hanging the tongue out of the side of the mouth
- Hesitant or reluctant to move smoothly under saddle
- Bucking under saddle
- Rearing
- Rushing, under saddle, in attempt to 'get away' from the pain/annoyance
- Rushing, balking when led in-hand
- If he can: moving away from our influence

E: Signs of a horse acting in self-defense
- Leaving our presence is the first choice; but if that is not possible:
- Biting
- Striking with front leg
- Kicking with hind leg
- Charging
- Rearing (if forward movement is blocked)

Some horses have learned through experience that 'the best defense is a good offense', either in response to a predator or perceived predator-like actions by humans.

Quite often these sorts of behaviors are interpreted by people as a horse challenging them or showing 'disrespect'. When really, the horse is simply being a horse and responding in the only way he can when he is in pain or thinks that his life is in danger.

Horses don't understand punishment. They interpret aggressive and violent action by people as a predator attempting to capture, corner and eat them.

F: Excitement

Excitement has its own body language:
- Head & tail go up
- The whole body becomes 'bouncy'
- The horse strongly needs to move his feet

It is usually an adrenalin rush based on novelty or enthusiasm rather than fear. A combination of excitement and anxiety can see the tail very high (even straight up with some horses) and the horse becomes unusually 'large'.

The key to being with horses is to understand how to be assertive, like another herd member is assertive, without being aggressive.

If a horse is using body language so strong that we fear for our safety, that horse has not been educated to be able to have positive interactions with people. The fault lies with the people, not the horse.

We put the horse in a position of captivity and expect him to get used to all sorts of things he would never encounter in the wild.

When we use ropes and small pens, we have removed the horse's primary way of feeling safe again – the ability to move away and re-assess a situation.

Most training systems don't allow the horse to move far enough away or give him the time he needs to make decisions about whether something is dangerous or harmless.

Educating the horse with reward reinforcement (food rewards as in Clicker Training) uses his natural curiosity and endless appetite for something tasty.

It seems a good way to proceed. If you are interested in finding out more about Clicker Training, please see my book, *How to Begin Equine Clicker Training.*

Unless challenged and unable to move away, horses by nature are peace-loving and co-operative unless shortage of food and water cause serious stress.

31. The Expressive Parts of the Horse

Although we obviously have to look at each expressive part in context with what the horse's whole body is saying, it can be helpful to look at the parts individually.

31-1: Ears

Ears could be categorized as:

Alert — forward, scanning in anxious mode

Curious/Interested — forward with head movement up or down to focus the eyes

Attentive — forward to what is going on

Back/Sideways - Anxious — only the context of the situation and the rest of the horse's body language can tell us if the ears are back due to anxiety (very stiff), or back because the horse is strongly focusing on a task (not as stiff)

Back/Sideways - Floppy — a chilled out, resting or casually moseying along horse often has the ears half back in a relaxed state.

Pinned — truly pinned ears are a very strong signal that all is not well and other action will follow if things don't change immediately. Some horses lay their ears almost flat when they are strongly focusing on a complex task. This can be more like a 'frown' of concentration and we have to be careful not to presume the ears are pinned and take evasive/inhibitory action that will confuse the horse who was just busy thinking his way through a problem.

It pays to give the horse the benefit of any doubt and read the overall situation and body language rather than just the ears. *Truly pinned ears are unmistakable*, once seen. They are usually accompanied by a very angry face overall and are often followed by snaky-neck movement toward the cause of annoyance.

Working Ears: Back or Sideways, - Focused/Thinking — some horses put their ears to the back or side when they are in 'thinking' mode.

We often see these sorts of ear positions in horses doing their 'job' of the moment; e.g., cutting horses, calf-roping horses, dressage horses, horses doing an Agility course.

Because they are carrying out a learned pattern in a known environment, their mind is focused on the task at hand and the precise signals coming from their handler. Their ears often resemble the ears of a dog working sheep. Back and full of concentration on the job.

The ears may resemble that of an irritated or disgruntled horse but if the horse is doing his 'job' and his overall tension and body expression suggest that he is focused, we are probably seeing his personal 'working' expression.

Often, as soon as the horse has finished a part of his 'job', the ears pop forward before the next obstacle or cow or whatever.

It's helpful to watch video clips focusing just on the horse's ears. Usually they are constantly in motion and give us an insight into what may be going on in the horse's mind. Obviously, we can never be sure, but we can get a good idea.

Each horse's ear expressions will follow the same general pattern, but at the same time be unique, so we should be careful about generalizing too much between horses.

Figure 32: Alert ears with a moderately raised head.
She is watching someone on the road.

Figure 33: Curious Ears, moving head to get best focus through the trifocal lens (see Part 2-1).

Figure 34: Attentive Ears, head level with withers.

Figure 35: Sideways ears quite tight, giving an anxious expression. Note the relatively tight lips.

Figure 36: Back/Sideways Ears, relaxed; note the relaxed lower lip.

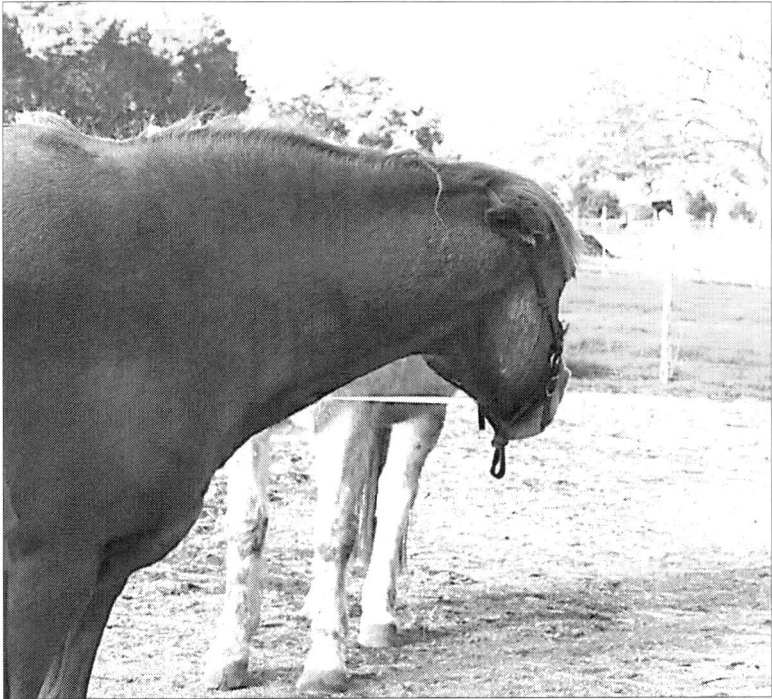

Figure 37: Truly pinned ears giving a clear message to Smoky.

Figure 38: Working Ears, back but focused and thinking

Figure 39: These ears may look pinned, but they are this mare's focused working ears during a demanding task.

Figure 40: Another example of sideways, thinking ears.

Figure 41: One ear focused on handler, the other focused on the next obstacle.

A: A bit more about ears

It's interesting to note ear differences between mares and geldings/stallions.

Recently I watched YouTube clips of the Pignon brothers Frederic and Jean-Francois. Frederic and his wife, Magali Delgado, were the original stars of Cavalia (2003-2009).

Below is the link if you would like to watch Frederic playing with three of his young stallions.

https://youtu.be/w1YO3j-Zh3g (accessed 03.04.15)

In another clip, Jean-Francois Pignon played with a troupe of mares.

https://youtu.be/qncbDfT5KsU (accessed 29.03.15)

I didn't know they were mares when I first watched it, but their behavior was so different from that of Frederic's stallions, I presumed they were mares. The message was in the ears.

The mares were constantly using their ears to maintain their individual bubbles while performing their routines which often had them very close together.

Mares in a natural herd situation determine much of the social structure of their group. Social order within a group needs a ready language with all sorts of nuances. Mare's ears have these nuances.

Mares' job of giving birth and caring for their foals means that they need to cultivate detailed knowledge of their environment.
- Best grazing spots
- Safe water
- The nature and habits of the local predators
- Health of the herd stallion
- Bachelor groups in the vicinity
- Intrinsic awareness of their present rank in the group of mares

Horses give way to horses above them in rank, and they expect horses lower in rank to give way to them. Mares need to keep track of lots of things.

Mares have a full complement of hormones and hormonal cycles. In wild herds, their position in the herd is closely linked with survival of themselves and their offspring during the annual hard times of summer drought and winter cold and snow.

We often like to romanticize wild horses, but there is not much romantic about a life lived in the environmental margins of the deserts, plains and mountains where they manage to survive.

Having had mares and geldings, I have found a distinct difference. All other things being equal (which they never are) mares tend to be more independent-minded, geldings more easy-going. That's a generalization, but it's not a coincidence that Cavalia™ uses only geldings and stallions for their shows.

The Ear Test:

If we can easily bend the tip of the ear, the horse is generally relaxed. If the ear is too stiff to bend, it signals that the horse has tension in his whole body and lacks confidence or is anxious at the moment.

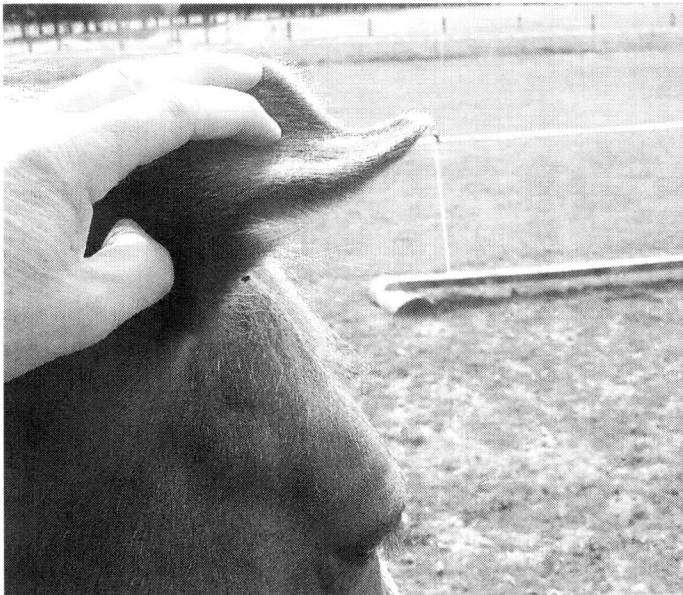

Figure 42: The Ear Test: how easily we can bend the tip of the ear is a good indicator of the horse's overall tension or relaxation.

Ears, it seems, can give a large range of signals, ranging from curiosity, acceptance, concentration, irritation, dominance and submission. All we have to do is work out which is which and when, for each horse in our life!

B: Ears and Horse Character Type

The fine points about how a specific horse uses his ears may also relate, to some extent, to the innate character type of the horse.

We can never put horses into labelled pigeonholes, but often it is helpful to describe what we see and create categories so we can communicate our descriptions more easily.

One way of categorizing horse character types is to look at their tendency to move their feet. A strong need to move suggests an extroverted character type. Less tendency to move suggest a more introverted character.

Another way of looking at horse character types is to note whether the horse is innately bold and curious or if he tends to stay out of the limelight and easily becomes anxious.

Quite likely, an *extroverted bold* horse will want to know where the party is and get going with it. He'll often show forward, inquisitive ears. If the handler is not providing fun, he is inclined to create fun for himself.

An *extroverted but anxious* type of horse, who tends to weigh up the cost/benefit of every situation, may have ears moving through many expressions.

An *introverted bold, imaginative* horse is usually most interested in the next blade of available grass. He sees little reason to move if his life is not in danger. He is strongly committed to his own ideas. He will learn things happily enough if we make it worth his while.

Such a horse tends to love food reward reinforcement and easily becomes a Clicker Training star. Once he learns something, he likes to make it his idea. He then tries hard to 'get it right'. His focus on his work may often include ears lying back or sideways as he thinks his way through the puzzle we've given him.

An *introverted anxious* type of horse may have active ears regularly checking out all points of the compass. He may appear externally 'quiet' but is heaving with emotions inside. Horses like this may suddenly 'explode', so it is important to identify them and keep a close eye on their comfort zone of the moment.

These are generalizations but generalizations can help give us an overview. Ears are obviously highly personalized for each horse. In new situations horses behave differently than they do at home, just as we do.

What I want to highlight is that it is easy to simplify how ears should look on a 'happy horse' when we really have little idea of what is going on in the horse's mind and being expressed in his ears.

We should always read ears in the context of the rest of the horse's body and the specific situation of the moment.

A horse in an enclosed space with little stimulation will have different ear expressions than the same horse out and about with a wide view of things going on all around him.

31-2: Tails

If we want to describe tail activity, we can mention:
- *Relaxed at rest*: the tail hangs straight down unless swishing flies.
- *Jaunty and relaxed in motion*: the tail is raised slightly, usually indicating the horse is relatively relaxed and comfortable with the work he is doing. It swings rhythmically with the horse's movement.
- *Twitching*: some horses give a little twitch in response to receiving and accepting a new signal from the handler.
- *Swishing*: often a signal, when learning something new, of opposition reflex or concern with the request. It signals that there is some physical, mental and/or emotional discomfort to work through.

- *Wringing*: this is often seen in horses doing a dressage test as they work through the discomfort of the situation.
- *Clamped*: the dock of the tail is held tightly against the flank. It is a clear signal that the horse is tense in his whole body and mind. It is impossible to put ones hand under the tail to rub and make it rise, so this is another excellent 'tension test'.
- *J-shaped Clamping*: the tail is held so tightly that it is literally a J-shape. I've only seen this on video where an un-handled horse was being hazed in a round pen. It probably signals terror in the horse's mind, that death is imminent.

The tail is as expressive as the ears and jaw/chin. Often, we are not in a position to notice subtle tail signals such as the slight twitch. The best way to learn tail language is to watch video clips. In fly season, it gets even trickier.

The Tail Test

We can use this like the 'ear test' mentioned earlier. If rubbing under the tail causes the horse to lift the tail, he is relaxed emotionally and mentally. If the tail clamps down, it signals that the horse is holding physical, emotional and/or mental tension.

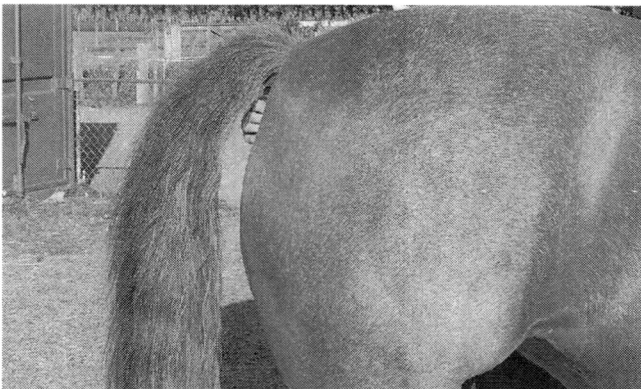

Figure 43: The Tail Test: if we rub under the horse's tail and he easily lifts his tail, the horse is nicely relaxed.

31-3: Jaw/Chin

The jaw and chin also give us information about the horse's state of mind and emotion. Because horses don't have a lot of facial muscles, we have to be especially attentive to the ears, the set of the jaw, and the tension in the chin or lower lip area. It takes awareness to become conscious of differences in the jaw. We can take note of the jaw/chin in the following ways.

- In neutral — we can easily gently flip the bottom lip away from the teeth
- Very tense — chin feels like a rock (the extreme in a continuum of tension)
- Very relaxed — lower lip flops on its own

Jaw Actions: Lip-licking, Chewing & Yawning

Horses appear to *lick* and *chew* after they've thought their way through a situation and are 'processing' it in their mind. I wonder if the term, 'chewing it over' comes from the era when horses lived closely with people and horsemen noticed this behavior.

Figure 44: Licking and Chewing

In Figure 44 Smoky is adjusting his mind to the fact that Lynette only wants to sit and relax: he doesn't need to do anything other than be polite. Being a friendly, touchy-feely horse, his natural tendency is to push, nuzzle and lick, so just relaxing and doing 'nothing' is a mental shift for him.

Like we hold tension in our shoulders, neck, furrowed brow (or indeed in our jaw if we tend to grind our teeth), horses hold tension in their jaws, so the licking and chewing is probably a conscious release of that tension.

Figure 45: This looks like a moderately tense lower lip/jaw.

Figure 46: Same horse, a much more relaxed lower lip/jaw than in the previous photo.

Yawning seems to be a way horses can release overall tension from their bodies.

Figure 47: Yawning seems to be a way of releasing whole-body tension.

31-4: Rapid Blinking

When a horse figures something out under pressure, it is often accompanied by very rapid blinking. There may be licking and chewing as well, so unless we are consciously looking for the blinking, it is easy to miss. I sometimes pick it up on video, having not noticed it while out with the horse.

Rapid blinking is a signal to the handler that the horse can use downtime to mentally digest what has just happened.

32. Individual Education Programs

The more carefully we thin-slice the task we want to set our horse, the easier it is for us to present new learning in a way the horse can understand.

The eight Training Plans included in the book can be used as starting points for creating Individual Education Programs (IEPs) for a particular horse.

The topics for the Training Plans are:

1. Walking Cleanly Over a Rail (Part 32-2)
2. Backing Over a Rail (Part 32-3)
3. Follow for Confidence (Part 33-7)
4. Relaxed Foot Care (Part 33-8)
5. Rope Texting (Part 33-9)
6. One Step at a Time (Part 33-10)
7. Head Down and Head Up (Part 33-11)
8. Light Rope/Rein Response (Part 33-12)

32-1: Acquisition

Acquisition includes getting our head around how we will teach a new behavior and then explaining it to the horse.

The way we first present new material is crucial. As much as possible, we want the horse to be continuously successful.

It's helpful to practice our ideas and techniques first on a person standing in for the horse. If you are lucky enough to have one, it also helps to work out techniques with an experienced horse before moving on to a novice horse.

Even a well-educated, experienced horse appreciates learning new things in small slices. This allows him to build confidence and expertise with each step toward being able to carry out the whole task smoothly.

The first step is to experiment a bit to see what the horse is already able to offer. We may decide to dwell on some of the basic elements in our Individual Education Program (IEP) to get them better. We might find some major training holes that need to be addressed.

For example, before asking our horse to walk cleanly over rails, as in Training Plan 1 below, have we taught him to walk confidently with us in Leading Position Three (beside his neck)?

32-2: Training Plan 1: Walking Cleanly over Rails

If the task I want to teach is walking over rails without touching them, my first slices would evolve around exercises to ensure that the horse has the gymnastic ability to lift his feet high enough to clear the rails as he steps over. Things like:

a) Walking up and down slopes forwards and backwards (can use mats for destination rest/click points to maintain enthusiasm).

b) We can add variety to this exercise by asking for 6 forward steps up the slope followed by 3 backward steps on the slope, and so on, playing with different numbers of steps. And do same heading down a slope.

For the exercises below we release/relax/rest (click&treat) if there are no touches.

If the horse touches the rail with a foot, *walk a loop and repeat* until the horse does it with no touches. Each loop is a re-set of the exercise. When you get a loop with no touches, celebrate hugely and go away to rest or do something easy.

I would start first with one element (one rail, one half barrel or one raised rail) and stay with it until I get no touches. Then add in another, stay with two until we get no touches, and so on until we can do a series of 4-6 with no touches.

c) Stepping over half barrels or small barrels or rail piles and 'logjams' where he has to really think and stretch and lift his shoulder and hocks
d) Walking over rails
e) Trotting over rails
f) Walking over raised rails or cavaletti
g) Trotting over rails or cavaletti
h) A circuit of a variety of the above at walk
i) A circuit of a variety of the above at trot

32-3: Training Plan 2: Backing over a Rail

A task to follow on from teaching the horse to step cleanly over rails could be to have him back his feet over a rail without touching it (popular Horse Agility obstacle).

If the horse is not already comfortable backing up straight for ten steps with a very light signal, there is little point in asking him to back over a rail. (See Training Plan 6, *One Step at a Time* in Part 33-10.)

Backing over a rail might involve teaching a 'lift' foot signal. A clicker savvy horse could learn to 'lift' by raising his knee to bump a target.

Otherwise, if I am using release reinforcement only, I could tap the leg and stop tapping when the foot lifts. Once the horse understands the task, I can add verbal and gesture signals to ask for a lifted foot. I can use the same verbal signal when I do foot care. The same signal may work to ask for extra lift when stepping back over the rail.

With a clicker savvy horse, I could also use modelling by exaggerating the lift of my knees when I ask him to step over the rail. That can work if we are facing the horse or if we are stepping over the rail beside him.

Goal behavior

Visualize what you would like: *I would like the horse to confidently back all four feet over a rail on the ground when I give a light 'back-up' signal.*

Each of the following slices is a release/click&treat point.

1. Back-up straight through a lane of ground rails; 10 or more steps
2. Back-up straight, ten or more steps, on a light signal, in a variety of situations
3. Back down gentle slopes
4. Back up gentle slopes
5. Walk across a tarp, carpet or board (maybe toward a pre-set destination)
6. Walk onto a tarp, carpet or board and halt and relax
7. Back onto a tarp or carpet or board, halt and relax
8. Back right across a tarp, carpet or board in a relaxed manner
9. Walk over a rail in both directions
10. Halt with the rail under his belly and relax
11. Back just the front feet over the rail and relax
12. Back toward the rail; halt/relax with the hind feet at the rail but not over it
13. Walk over the rail first, halt, then back hind feet over the rail; halt, walk forward again
14. Walk over the rail first, then back all four feet over the rail

15. Line up to back all four feet over the rail without stepping over the rail first
16. As 15 plus back only the hind feet over the rail; relax; walk forward
17. As 15 plus back all four feet over the rail without touching the rail; relax
18. Back one hind foot over the rail and relax in that position; relax; walk forward
19. And any other combination you can think of
20. Generalize to different venues, different rails, work on right side and left side of horse
21. Trot over the rail, then back over it
22. Different handler orientations to the horse.

Figure 49: Boots is carefully backing all four feet over the rail. I am in the 'shoulder-to-shoulder position, walking backwards as she walks backwards.

The Individual Education Program (IEP) based on a thin-sliced Training Plan like the one above should factor in the:

- Handler's body orientation for each slice
- Signals that the handler will use for each slice
- Environmental props that could be used to make it easier for the horse to understand what we want, e.g. guide rails, a lane or barrels either end of the rail so stepping over it makes more sense to the horse
- What the horse understands already
- How we will organize learning opportunities for the horse?
- When will it be good enough?

Note that the Training Plan above did not factor in handler orientation. The easiest way to teach backing is by turning to face the horse. (See Training Plan 6, *One Step at a Time* in Part 33-10.)

We can also teach backing by staying shoulder-to-shoulder with the horse and walking backwards as he backs up as in Figure 49. This method is a bit harder. The importance lies in choosing one and teaching it well before changing our orientation.

32-3: Fluency

Once we have written an Individual Education Program and carefully taken the horse through it, he will have acquired a new behavior.

If it is something that is part of daily general care and recreation, such as safe behavior around gates, the horse will have ample opportunity to use the new behavior often and receive reinforcement for it. His response to the signal will continue to become more fluent.

If, on the other hand, the new behavior is for a specific purpose, such as loading onto a trailer or trotting through a tunnel for Horse Agility, we have to set up special training opportunities to allow the horse to become fluent.

In my experience, if we train a new behavior to the point of fluency, the horse tends to remember it forever.

After my horse became fluent in navigating an S-bend of rails on the ground, I did not have to teach that obstacle again every time it was part of a Horse Agility course.

If a behavior is unreliable, it was not originally taught to the point of fluency.

32-4: More about Generalization

Once the horse understands a new task or a new skill, it is important to 'take it out into the world'. That is what I mean by 'generalization'. Through generalization, the horse gains further fluency with a task.

Generalization includes:

1. Asking for the behavior in different places but still at home
2. Using different props
3. Working at different times of the day
4. Working with a different handler (who uses the same signals)
5. Asking for the behavior away from home
6. Working with unusual distractions
7. Working at a different gait
8. Using a different body orientation
9. Fading out a signal and replacing it with a new one
10. If we are using Clicker Training, moving to occasional click&treat rather than each time we ask for the behavior.

Generalization helps the horse put the new learning into his long-term memory. Each time we quietly repeat the task, we help build the horse's confidence. If the horse is unable to do the task in a specific situation, it gives us a clue about where we are in our Education Program with this horse for this task.

33. Six More Training Plan Examples

We'll look at six more Training Plans that can be turned into Individual Education Programs for your horse.

Each horse and handler partnership is unique, so only the horse's handler can write a horse's Individual Education Program.

Before heading into the Training Plans, we'll review some more key ideas.

Ideally, we want to teach in a way that keeps the horse being continually successful. We want the horse to maintain his confidence with each part of the teaching/learning process.

We can do this using release reinforcement alone, or add in reward reinforcement via Clicker Training. A clicker savvy horse will learn very quickly.

Release reinforcement alone relies on the expert timing of the release. It can be harder for the horse because he is not motivated to actively seek what we want in order to earn a treat.

When we begin to use reward reinforcement on top of release reinforcement the handler makes a big mental shift.

Positive reinforcement causes the handler to look for *click points* to reward. It means we stop looking for things to correct. It is a huge shift in how we view our training.

If the horse is not responding in the way we want, we re-set the task, slice it thinner, until we find a slice so thin that the horse can't possibly get it wrong. Our slices have to be thin enough for the horse to understand and respond in the direction we are looking for.

This is what natural horsemanship practitioners call 'rewarding the slightest try'. *Releasing pressure at the slightest try is a hard skill to master because without a lot of experience, we don't know what the 'slightest try' feels like.*

Clicking at the first sign of what we want is much easier. The click&treat dynamic is also much more forgiving because *the horse is keenly seeking to understand what we want, not hoping to avoid a correction.*

If no click is forthcoming, most horses will keep trying to find out what will elicit the click&treat. In other words, the horse will understand that if there is no click, he hasn't yet cracked the puzzle.

We don't have to 'correct'. We only have to re-set the task to give him another opportunity to find the *click point* we want. The absence of the click is all the information the horse usually needs. *This is natural motivation that can't be achieved any other way.*

Horses always do the best they can, given the situation they are in. As we get better at understanding their perception of reality, our training will be more empathetic.

We'll take better note of what the horse is actually doing or trying to tell us. The horse's responses or reactions tell us where our focus has to be at each precise moment.

As an ideal coach for our horse, we are always on the lookout for:

1. increasing fluency as a new task is learned
2. relaxation and calmness
3. balance throughout the task
4. positive energy brought to the task.

All of the above can earn a release of signal pressure (click&treat).

As well as comfort from the release of the signal pressure and a reliable food reward when we use Clicker Training, many horses begin to enjoy the attention and the mental stimulation of the puzzles we teach them to solve.

We can enrich their environment and alleviate, to a small degree, the endless boredom of life in captivity.

The Training Plans presented here can be used as a springboard to create Individual Education Programs (IEPs) that suit your immediate purpose for a particular horse.

Soon you will be experimenting with your horse and outlining your own Training Plans to turn into Individual Education Programs.

33-1: A bit of terminology

Release/click point refers to the specific movement or behavior we are looking for to reinforce with a release (click&treat). We need to be clear in our mind what will earn the release (click&treat) before we begin to communicate with the horse.

Learning frame of mind is what we want when we start a teaching/learning session. We want him interested in what we are doing, but not over-reactive or totally disinterested.

It's easy to pick when a horse is high on fear or excitement. Other signs of not being in a 'learning frame of mind' may not be so easy to pick up.

If the horse is dashing around in his enclosure or on the end of our rope, we have to give him time to run off his adrenalin so he can switch from his 'reactive' mind back into his thinking or 'responsive' mind.

A horse might become reactive because of fear or anxiety or commotion or excitement due to something going on with other horses in the vicinity.

When the horse has switched, for whatever reason, into his 'survival mode' mindset, all we can do is avoid collateral damage and wait for him to feel safe enough to stop, observe and think. The human survival response is the same. Our lifestyle just means we have less need to activate it very often.

At the other extreme, the horse might be so disinterested that he is not in a learning frame of mind. He might be too hungry, too hot or tired after a stormy restless night. He might be sore somewhere in his body or suffering from arthritis. Mares are often described as 'moody', perhaps related to hormonal rhythms.

A familiar warm-up routine is a good way to assess the horse's frame of mind. We can then decide whether to go ahead with our planned training, have a day off or do something enjoyable and relaxing together instead of 'training'.

Teaching Phase is when we first introduce our horse to a new task and give him ample opportunity to practice it over many short sessions and eventually in different places.

Often it is also part of our own teaching/learning phase, as we experiment with signals until we and the horse can reach an agreement that makes sense to both of us. Most signals evolve quite naturally out of the training process.

Fluency is when our signals are consistent and smooth. We no longer have to exaggerate our signals for the horse to understand our intent. Our signal is in our muscle memory and we don't have to think it through each time we want to use it.

The signal pressure has become information the horse knows how to deal with. The signal is now a two-way communication and can become quite subtle.

Consolidation and Generalization are achieved when our horse can confidently carry out our requests in new locations and new situations.

Maintenance means that we review the task on a regular basis if it is not something we do as part of daily care.

33-2: How We Introduce Something New is Critical

Ideally, we set it up so that:

- We have thin-sliced the task into its smallest teachable parts and have an idea of where the first *release/click points* will be.
- We have thought about which part of the horse's body we need to influence, and we've planned the signal(s) we'll use (energy levels, body posture, body position, gesture, touch, words, strong intent).
- The environment is set up to make it as easy as possible for the horse to understand what we want: e.g. use of a lane or a corner; where we place the mat target or a nose target; use of barriers on the far side of the horse; where we position our body.
- #39-#40 in my *HorseGym with Boots* provide detail about using lanes.

When we begin to teach a task with movement forward or back, we need to release (click&treat) the moment of 'lift-off', not the moment of completion. In other words, the foot lifting, not the foot setting down.

Once the horse understands the signals for 'walking on' or 'backing up' several steps, he'll soon learn that the release/click point can shift so it happens at the end of a series of movements.

Ideally, we make what we want easier for the horse to do than what we don't want. Setting up the training environment to achieve this means we are already halfway there.

If, instead, the horse learns evasive moves during our first fumbling with a new task, our Education Program has suddenly become more complex and longer. A bit of thoughtful planning can make things much easier for us and the horse.

Ideally, we try out our ideas with another person standing in as the horse. Or we can trial our process on a more experienced, forgiving horse, if we are lucky enough to have one. That helps us over the hurdle of the early trial and error.

It allows us to be clearer for the horse when we first introduce something new, rather than confuse him because we have not yet worked out a smooth way to proceed.

The first step is always to make sure the horse is relaxed and in a learning frame of mind. If something has brought up his adrenalin, we do calming procedures or something active until he's used up the adrenalin and can return to relaxation.

Or we wait to start the new thing in a later session. If he gets tense during a training session, we must return the horse and ourselves to relaxation before continuing.

We start teaching each slice of the whole task with *release/click points* determined by what the horse is able to offer already. As both horse and handler get smooth with each tiny slice, we gradually chain the slices together and shift the *release/click point* until the whole task can be achieved with one *release/click point* at the end.

When we begin teaching something new, we start by finding a beginning *release/click point*. For some things, this may be a very rough approximation of the final goal behavior, e.g. just a tiny drop of the head when we begin to teach head lowering right to the ground.

This is illustrated in the *Head Lowering* video clips in the *Free-Shaping* playlist.

We gradually shift the *release/click point* toward closer and closer approximations of what we want until we achieve the goal behavior.

Good timing of the release/click allows the horse to become more and more accurate.

When teaching something new, the focus of release (click&treat) is on the new learning, but we can still release (click&treat) good execution of things the horse already knows.

33-3: Re-setting a Task

When we teach something new, we are experimenting with our signals and the horse is also experimenting to work out what it is we want him to do. It's not unusual for things to get a bit complicated and messy.

If either you or the horse lose track of what you are doing, pretend it was perfect, relax (but no click&treat), pause. Then go back to the beginning of the task and try again, starting with your visualization of how a good effort will look and feel.

The magic about pretending it went well (when it actually turned into a mess) is that it dissolves the natural frustration we feel when our communication is not getting through.

If we can smile, breathe out and relax our body before the re-set, we don't upset the horse or make him anxious. We simply start again.

When someone tries to teach me a new computer program, they invariably go so fast that I have no idea what they did or what I should be doing. I think that is what often happens with horses.

33-4: Fluidity and Consolidation of New Learning

The *Consolidation Phase* begins when the horse generally understands our signal, our intent and usually responds willingly with the move we want.

At this point we can keep up interest and enthusiasm by providing an extra-long release time (or click&treat) whenever any part of the task is done really well.

To put a new task into long-term memory (for horses and for people) it needs to be practiced *at least* 9 or 10 sessions in a row; ideally over 9 or 10 days in a row. Some tasks will take longer, depending on their complexity. If we can't have a session every day, we need to accept that it will take longer to build a new behavior solidly. Keeping a written record becomes essential.

How many 'repeats' we should do during one session is hard to pin down because it depends so much on:

- What we are teaching
- The character type of the horse (and handler)
- Age, history and health of the horse
- What the horse knows already
- The skill of the handler
- The nature of the handler-horse relationship.
- How well the handler can stay calm and empathetic.

In some cases, if the horse does something correctly and we ask him to do it again because we 'want to practice', the horse will think he did it wrong the first time and try something else.

If we want to practice something to improve our own gear handling or timings skills, we should ideally ask another person to stand in for the horse, or use a more experienced horse if we have one.

If the horse's first effort is really good, it is probably better to do something else and come back to do another 'practice' later in the session.

One possible 'rule of thumb' is the 'Rule of Three'. It consists of three practice repeats in a row, unless the first one is perfect and calls for a major celebration.

If the horse is in the learning stage, each tiny improvement over last time is a good 'release/click point', followed by doing something else the horse finds easy.

During the overall training session, we could return to the new task three times, doing other familiar things in-between.

Vanessa Bee has written a book about teaching new things over many tiny sessions three minutes long. I've done this, and it works well.

33-5: Thin-Slicing Revisited

Thin-slicing was the topic of Part 8 but this is a good spot to review the key points.

1. Write down the over-all task you'd like to achieve.
2. Brainstorm to break the whole task into the smallest teachable/clickable slices that you can think of.
3. Organize the slices into an order that makes sense to you.
4. Have a low-intensity play with your horse to see which of the slices he can already offer. This gives you a starting point for writing the Individual Education Program (IEP) for that particular horse.
5. Consider the character type, age, health, background experience of your horse and set out an IEP. Start with what the horse can already do, and organize the slices into an order that might suit that horse best.
6. Consider how often you can train. If your horse lives at your place and you can pop out three times a day for a mini-session, things can progress rapidly. If your horse is boarded and you see him daily, things can also progress rapidly. If you can only visit your horse once a week, things may go a bit more slowly. In other words, you need to add your 'opportunity' strand into your IEP (see Part 5: *Signal Opportunities*).
7. Work out where your release/click points will probably be for each slice. This can change once you actually begin with the horse. Feedback from the horse and your own reactions will always affect what you do next.
8. The main idea is to keep the horse being successful as much as possible. If an attempt gets fluffed up (by you or the horse), pause, relax and re-set the mini-skill (slice) you are working on. As long as the horse is willing to try again, nothing is lost. If we get frustrated the horse feels it in a nanosecond and will become anxious.

9. As mentioned elsewhere, a good way to avoid that feeling of frustration is to 'pretend' it went well, which can make us smile and makes it easier to relax and calmly re-set the task.
10. The IEP is a dynamic document that gets tweaked and changed around. It is always a 'work in progress'.
11. What works for one horse may not work for another, so each horse needs his own IEP.
12. It's easy to have too few slices in our IEP but we can never have too many. The easier the horse can move from tiny slice to tiny slice, the easier it is for him to be continually successful and wanting to do more. Success builds on success.

Successive Approximations

In simple English, this means that we start with what the horse can offer already and gradually direct and reward each tiny change in the direction of the final behavior we want.

In other words, at the beginning of teaching something new, we release (click&treat) for the slightest approximation of what we want as our final result. Each approximation becomes one slice of the overall task.

Each time the horse feels ready, we encourage him to do a tiny bit more to gain the release (click&treat). This whole process of rewarding successive approximations is called 'shaping' a behavior.

A human example of 'shaping a behavior' is teaching a child to write. We start with holding a pencil and using it to make random marks on paper. At some point the random marks become conscious curves and straight lines.

When the time is right, we introduce writing the letters of the alphabet. Eventually the child can group letters to make words. Words are then arranged into meaningful sentences. Some children go on to write coherent paragraphs, essays, stories or books.

If the child loses confidence with any of the 'slices' of the process, an element of discomfort can creep in, along with typical avoidance behavior. Not enough practice then results in a poorly shaped skill.

Writing is an interesting human endeavor that starts at two years old and is still in formative stages ten years later.

Another way to look at successive approximations is to think of a sculptor starting with a piece of stone. He works in careful stages until the shape in his mind is visible to the rest of us in the shape of the sculpture.

In the same way, we gradually tease a series of movements (or stillness) out of a horse to yield a complete task. This is a bit harder than shaping stone because horses have a mind of their own.

33-6: General Reminders

1. The faster you take the pressure off (click&treat), the faster the horse can learn to recognize just what it is you want.
2. Once the horse knows the task, always start with the lightest signal possible then add energy and intent until you get a prompt response.
3. If you keep nagging with light signals you will desensitize the horse and make him dull to the signal. It is an easy habit to get into and hard to break.
4. For each horse, you have to experiment with the amount of energy (intensity) your signal needs to get the desired response. For sensitive, anxious horses, it might be very little.
5. A bold, strong-minded horse might need stronger signal pressure at first while he works out that you won't back off because he is resisting. It is essential to lessen the signal pressure as soon as the horse complies.

6. The energy you need to apply will also change with the situation and what you are asking the horse to do.

7. One of the key skills of horsemanship is to read the horse accurately to be able to decide on the best signal to use at any one moment. It is part of the concept of *feel*.

8. Just when everything is feeling really good is the time to STOP. Avoid at all costs the urge to 'do it again to see if we can'. Go do something relaxing instead.

33-7: Training Plan 3: Follow for Confidence

As we mentioned in the section on Environmental Signals, horses seem to have a natural tendency to follow anything moving away from them. They also move away from anything coming toward them.

People tend to approach a horse with a new thing to 'show it to them'. Since horses instinctively move away from anything unusual coming toward them, this does not set the scene for instilling confidence.

If we are introducing something new to the horse, we can make it much easier by walking away with it first and allowing the horse to follow as far behind as he needs, to feel safe. When he's ready, he will approach and put his nose on the object.

Aim:

To allow the horse to 'discover' a new object in a way that allows him time to explore, experiment, and make up his own mind that the new object is harmless.

Environment:
- Work in a space familiar to the horse, where he is usually relaxed.
- We can do it at liberty in a safe, enclosed area, or we can have a long rope or lunge line on the horse.

- Ensure he is in a learning frame of mind. If not, encourage activity to use up adrenalin or relax or play with things he knows to overcome anxiety, before starting.
- With a new object like a wheelbarrow, bike, tractor or dragging rope, we need a helper to move in front of us with the object so we can follow along with the horse.

The new object might be:
- Wheelbarrow moving
- Saddle pad
- Saddle
- Halter
- Tarp or horse cover
- Dragging rope
- Bag on a stick
- String on a stick
- Umbrella
- Bicycle moving
- Tractor moving
- Pebbles rattling in a plastic bottle
- Rope dragging pebbles in a plastic bottle
- Rope dragging a branch or a tree
- Massager
- Spray bottle
- Flags
- Flashlight (lamp, torch) in the dark
- Big ball moving

Method:

The nature of the item will dictate whether we can walk away with our back to the horse to begin with. Walking away with our back to the horse is useful because horses perceive our energy as coming from our core (belly button area), so it is easier for the horse to relax and get curious if we are not facing him, but holding the object behind our back.

If we have a helper walking away with the new object, we can follow with the horse wearing halter and lead. At some point, we ask our helper to slow down so the horse can get closer. Then we ask them to stop so the horse can put his nose near or on the object.

Figure 50: If a horse is worried about a new object, having it move away so the horse can follow it is the ideal way to allow the horse to build confidence in his own time.

The idea is to walk the object away, being mindful of when the horse shows *interest* to target the object. At first, any sign of curiosity is a release/click point. When the horse appears comfortable with the new item (and we are working without a helper) we turn around to face the horse and walk backwards so we can easily see when he'd like to put his nose on it for a release (click&treat).

We can use a dragging rope, with a five-liter white plastic container attached, as an example.

'Walking Away' is illustrated in *#21-#22. HorseGym with Boots.* The way we did it in video clip *#22* (from 2:39 mark) with Smoky at liberty was a lot of fun.

With a spooky or anxious horse, it may be better to start with just a long rope first and a helper to walk dragging the rope so the horse and handler can follow it together.

Release/click points could be:

1. When the horse shows an interest in the dragging rope
2. When he puts his nose on the end of the rope (or container if using one).

When the horse is calm and ho-hum about following the rope, our release/click point can change to:

3. Horse standing still while we walk around him dragging the rope
4. Have halter and lead on, ask the horse to walk with the handler who is dragging the rope. Release/click points are any sign of relaxation. Video clip #22 clearly shows how anxious Smoky was at first
5. Build in 'halt' and 'walk on', still dragging the rope, until it is ho-hum

Generalization:
6. Repeat 4 and 5 above with the handler walking on the horse's other side
7. Drag the rope on different surfaces (start again with Slice 1)

In the clip you can see that the noise of the container on the sand caused anxiety. So we went back to Slice 1 and worked through all the steps again on the sand. It didn't take long to regain Smoky's confidence on the new surface. He realized it was only a different noise. This is an example of changing a parameter to 'generalize' a task.

This Training Plan can be adapted to any new item we want to introduce to our horse.

Quick Summary about Creating an Individual Education Program

To create the Individual Education Program for a specific horse, we work through the following steps.

- We experiment to see what the horse already knows or thinks.
- We brainstorm a list of the smallest teachable parts (slices) of the whole task
- We put the slices into an order that makes sense to us and hopefully the horse
- We learn and teach any individual skills that may be missing
- We continually tweak and change the program as we get feedback from self and horse

In short, we can think of this as a cycle of:

Plan Program -- Do – Observe (self and horse) – Contemplate new feedback – Tweak Program, and so on, forever until we have smooth execution of the overall task.

33-8: Training Plan 4: Relaxed Foot Care

Aim:

The horse confidently lifts each foot on signal and keeps it up for as long as we need it.

Environment:
- Work in a space familiar to the horse, where he is usually relaxed.
- Have halter and lead on the horse.

- I prefer to have the horse with halter and lead rope, but not tied, as it gives him more leeway to express his feelings. If the horse can't stand quietly without being tied, that could be a good skill to work on first. Giving the horse a mat as a destination spot for standing quietly can be helpful.
- *#6-#12 HorseGym with Boots* inclusive are all about using mats.
- We can work alone or have a relaxed, confident person holding the horse. If you don't have the help of a *relaxed, confident* person, working alone may be easier for the horse (and you).
- Ensure the horse is in a learning frame of mind. If not, encourage activity to use up adrenalin or relax and play with things he knows to overcome anxiety before starting.

It pays to remember that if you are nervous about picking up a horse's foot, your anxiety pales into insignificance compared with how worried a horse might be if he has not been introduced to foot care with thought to his feelings.

Horses know that if their feet are compromised, they are close to death. It pays to teach 'picking up feet' carefully and thoroughly and not leave it to other people.

Have the halter and a 10'-12' rope on your horse. Ask him to move his feet slightly until he is standing square. Training Plan 6, *One Step at a Time,* in Part 33-10, is helpful if the horse is not used to being asked to move his feet individually.

First make sure you can rub and massage all four legs down to the heel with the horse able to stand still in a relaxed manner, totally confident that you are not going to hurt him.

Figure 51: Bridget is using a feed bag over her body extension to make sure Smoky is fine with an unusual object running down his legs. She has one hand on his neck to catch any feeling of tension. She is keeping her head in a safe position while she checks out his responses.

Use advance and retreat. That means start at the withers and move down a leg until one of you feels uncomfortable. When you reach either you or the horse's threshold of comfort, retreat by moving your hand back up to the withers, relax, then advance again. This is called a *re-set*. You know you have reached a threshold if you feel tension in the horse's body or feel anxiety in your mind.

Every time we do a re-set we have a new opportunity to clarify our signal and our intent.

Stay close to the horse and keep your feet parallel to the horse's feet.

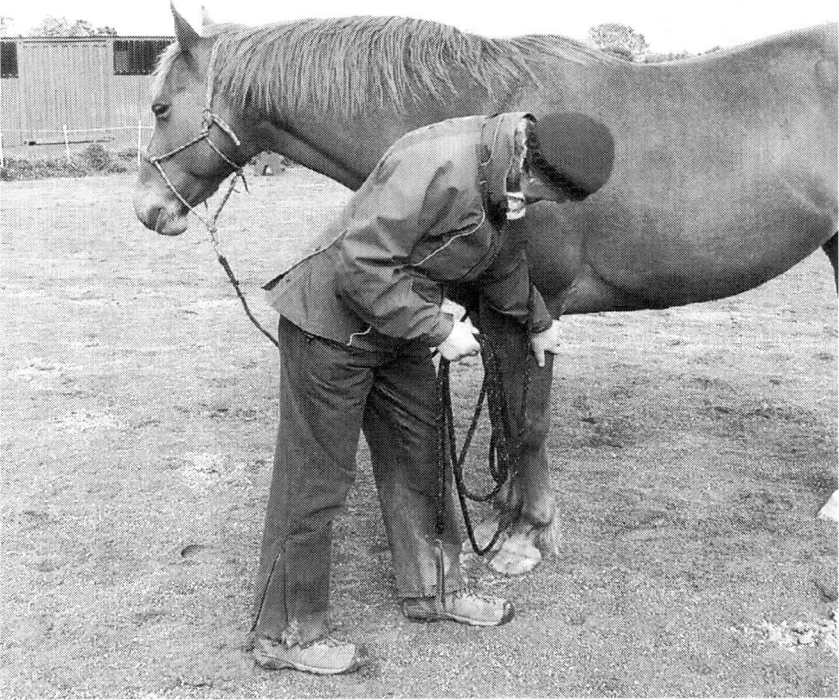

Figure 52: Bridget started with her hand at Boots' withers, and is in the process of running it down her leg to the chestnut to give the 'please pick up your foot' touch signal.

Before we can give the horse confidence about trusting his foot to our care, we have to build up our own confidence. The best way is to do it in short, 3-minute segments, working through a series of thin-sliced questions that might look like the list below.

You will be collecting feedback on how you feel about each slice, and how your horse feels about each slice. You stay with each slice until the answer to the question is, 'Yes.'

It could take five minutes to get all 'yes' answers with one horse. It could take a week or a month of brief 3-minute sessions to get all 'yes' answers with another horse.

For each approach, start at the withers and run your hand along and down to show the horse which leg you want to pick up. Once your horse understands this, it gives him time to shift his weight so he can pick up the foot. Expect to teach this whole process four times, once for each foot. The horse may have a different emotional response for each foot.

A: Hind Feet

This example is about picking up the right hind foot.

1. *Can I:* gently & confidently rub his leg & foot all over with my body extension (stick, bag on a stick, pool noodle)? Practice on an experienced horse or a person to get the feel for it if this is new to you (see figure 51).
2. *Will my horse:* let me rub his leg and foot with my body extensions? Make sure he is already comfortable with being rubbed over the rest of his body.
3. *Can I:* confidently rub his leg & foot with my hand? Start at his withers and rub down only as far as you feel comfortable at that time. Over many tiny sessions, you will get the confidence to rub all the way down.
4. *Will my horse:* let me rub his leg and foot with my hand?
5. *Can I:* get him to stand so he will be balanced when I pick up that foot? Have I taught him how to move forward and back one step at a time? If not, teach that first (See Training Plan 6 in Part 33-10.)
6. *Can I:* confidently ask him to pick up his foot by pressing on the cap of his hock?
7. *Will my horse:* pick up his foot when I touch the cap of his hock?
8. *Will my horse:* take the weight off his right hind leg when I run my hand from his withers, along his back and down the right side of his butt?
9. *Can my horse:* keep his balance okay standing on three legs?
10. *Will my horse:* let me hold his foot for one second before getting tense and needing it back?

11. *Can I*: let my hand and arm holding the foot swing freely with any movement the horse makes with his leg until it stops swinging, at which point I gently release the foot? (I do this only if I'm feeling safe.)
12. *Will my horse*: gradually let me hold the foot longer and longer and stay relaxed?
13. *Will my horse*: hold his foot up in a relaxed way for as long as I need it up?

B: Front Feet

It's important to repeat this Education Program for every foot. For front feet, it works well to touch (maybe gently squeeze at first) the chestnut as a signal for lifting the foot. If you start at the withers each time, the horse will most likely soon have his weight shifted and his foot lifted when you reach the chestnut.

It can be handy to teach a concurrent verbal signal such as, 'Lift' if you intend to do Horse Agility where the horse is asked to step cleanly over a rail, forwards and backwards.

Some horses may have had a bad experience with a particular leg. Be aware that a reluctance to lift a foot or keep it up can be due to pain from an old injury, current sore muscles/joints or arthritis.

I like to do foot care after the horse is nicely warmed up, since warmed up muscles will find the strain of standing on three legs easier.

33-9: Training Plan 5: Rope Texting and Backing-Up

The way we handle the rope can be compared to sending a text with our phone. There is someone on the other end of the rope or phone, receiving our message.

Text messages can be affectionate, informative and helpful. They can also be rude, cranky or abusive.

In other words, text messages can leave receivers confident, smiling and relaxed, or they can cause endless anxiety leading to emotional and mental break-down.

The way we transfer messages along the rope to our horse has a huge bearing on the way our horse perceives us. When I take my horse out walking, I frequently have to ask friendly people who 'love horses' to please not grab her rope and pull on it.

Many people view their halter and rope as a way of stopping their horse from 'leaving'. Sadly, this is often true. How much nicer to think of our halter and rope as a communication tool – a communication cable along which we can send a variety of messages.

When we have the horse in a rope and halter, we can send a signal down the rope to the halter. It allows us to 'touch' the horse from a distance. This can be a pretty spooky experience for a horse at first, so the more finesse we can put into the request, the better.

The horse may have previously learned one or both of the following.

1. If he pulls hard enough the rope will sometimes 'give' and he can get rid of the pressure
2. That no matter how hard he pulls, all he will get is a very sore head, neck and body, so he has 'given up' and lives with the anxiety of having his movement restricted

If the horse has this sort of background, building new sensitized rope-response habits will take longer and need careful attention.

Importance of the Back-Up

Knowing that we can ask the horse to back up in almost any situation adds a big plus to our safety rating.

By using reward reinforcement (click&treat) on top of our releases, and arranging the teaching environment to make it easy for the horse to understand what we are asking, we can build a nice willingness to back up with a variety of signals and different orientations of the handler's body.

Once the horse understands the signals in the teaching environment, we can carefully generalize them to different or new situations.

Having the horse respond readily to back up signals makes it easier to teach more complex movements, like yielding the shoulder into a turn on the haunches, because we can quickly let the horse know that forward movement is not what we want *without causing anxiety because we are suddenly throwing in extra signals which we have not previously taught.*

Horses feel everything. The more polite we can be with our rope handling, the more enchanted our horse will be about working with us. No one likes to feel grabbed around the head. By learning to *speak with the rope*, we can give the horse gentle notice about what is happening, giving him time to adjust his flexion and balance.

Aim:

To handle our rope in a way that sends a soft back-up signal along the rope to the halter.

Environment:
1. Prerequisites to this task are outlined in #27 *HorseGym with Boots* and in the *Backing Up* clip in my *Thin-Slicing Examples* playlist.
2. We want the horse to be comfortable backing up with a variety of signals before we look in more detail at this one.
3. The video that best accompanies this task is in the *Thin-Slicing Examples* playlist in a clip called *Rope Texting*
4. It helps to teach new things in an area with which the horse is already confident.
5. Set up a lane with raised rails on either side or have a safe fence on one side and a raised rail on the other side. Have it wide enough for the horse to walk through comfortably but not so wide that he can turn around. Detail about lanes is illustrated in *#39-#40 HorseGym with Boots.*

6. The handler walks on the outside of the lane; the horse walks inside the lane.
7. Have something ready to safely close off one end of the lane.
8. If the horse tells us that he can't do something, we immediately change our Individual Education Program to incorporate the prerequisites the horse needs to be successful with the task we have set. For example, if the horse is dubious about stepping into and through the lane we have set up, we would thin-slice that activity until the horse is totally cool with it. We might start with walking between two barrels and gradually make the sides of the lane longer and longer.
9. Halter and 10'-12' rope on the horse. The ideal rope for first teaching this is fairly thick yacht braid that easily transmits small movements to the halter. Webbing type ropes/lunge lines don't work well for teaching this but once the horse is sensitive to the signal, they work fine too.
10. To break up the intensity of new teaching/learning, include a relaxation mat if the horse is mat savvy, or an easy fun task in your plan to use after a series of efforts or after an especially good effort. This gives the horse time to soak in or digest what he has just accomplished with the new task. If the horse is still keen, return to the task or leave it until the next training session.
11. Knowing when to stop asking for something is just as important as knowing when to start asking for it.

Our training plan can be set up so we ask the horse a series of questions. Each of our thin slices can become a question. We stay with each question until the horse answers, "Yes, I can do that." Then we move on to the next question. Some horses will easily achieve all the questions in one training session.

Other horses will get stuck at certain points and need more time to reach their 'yes' answer. Generally, it is better to do a little bit often rather than push through the resistance. Doing a little bit often gives the horse ample time to reflect on the new signals and the new expected behaviors.

A little bit often creates a more solid foundation on which to build further lessons. The more solid the foundation, the more smoothly the sophisticated movements will follow. In other words, time spent on the foundation exercises is worth its weight in gold because we can easily build whatever we want on the solid foundation.

Very short lessons over several days is an easier way to train than forcing the issue which can result in emotional responses, opposition reflex, and create unwanted behaviors that end up making the whole teaching/learning process much more difficult than it needs to be.

It's often hard for people to give up our 'I want it now' mentality. Horses live in a different time frame. Their existence flows with the rising and setting of the sun, eating, drinking, social interaction, keeping cool or keeping sheltered as the seasons change. The more we can link into that timelessness, the easier the training will be on both sides of the rope.

Quality Control

If the horse can confidently indicate 'yes' three times in a row to a specific question, we have usually established 'quality control' and can move on to the next question.

In the teaching/learning stage, we release (click&treat) each correctly done 'slice' of the whole task. As the horse's understanding grows, the various stages of the task gradually become self-reinforcing and we can proceed with fewer release (click&treat) points. Eventually the horse will need only one release (click&treat) at the end of the whole task.

QUESTIONS TO ASK THE HORSE:

Are you able to confidently:

1. *Walk through* this lane with me in your right eye? Relax (click&treat), pause.
2. *Walk through* this lane with me in your left eye? Relax (click&treat), pause.
3. Walk into this lane with me in your right eye and *halt*? Relax (click&treat), pause, walk on out.
4. Walk into this lane with me in your left eye and *halt*? Relax (click&treat), pause, walk on out.
5. Walk into this *dead-end* lane with me in your right eye and halt? Relax (click&treat), pause.
6. Walk into this *dead-end* lane with me in your left eye and halt? Relax (click&treat), pause.
7. Walk into this *dead-end* lane, halt and back up if I *lift the rope straight up and gently jiggle* it as a signal for you to back up a step? [*Still moving back as the horse moves back.*] Relax (click&treat), pause. (See figure 53 below.)

Figure 53: Gentle wiggle on the rope held straight up is a signal for backing-up.

8. Walk into this *dead-end* lane, halt and back up if I gently *jiggle the rope from my waist level* as a signal for you to back up a step? Relax (click&treat), pause.

9. As 8 above but we can *back-up together* for several steps? Relax (click&treat), pause.

10. Without a lane, *stand quietly beside me shoulder-to-shoulder*, both of us relaxed? Relax (click&treat), pause.

11. Without a lane, walk with me *toward a fence and halt* facing the fence? Relax (click&treat), pause.

12. As 11 above plus back up straight when I gently jiggle the rope *from my waist level* as a signal? Relax (click&treat), pause.

13. Without a lane, stand quietly while I turn to face your shoulder, both of us relaxed? Relax (click&treat), pause. (See Figure 54.) *You may note that in the video clip I used a mat as an 'anchor point' for Boots. It is much easier for the horse when there are 'destination points' built into a larger task.*

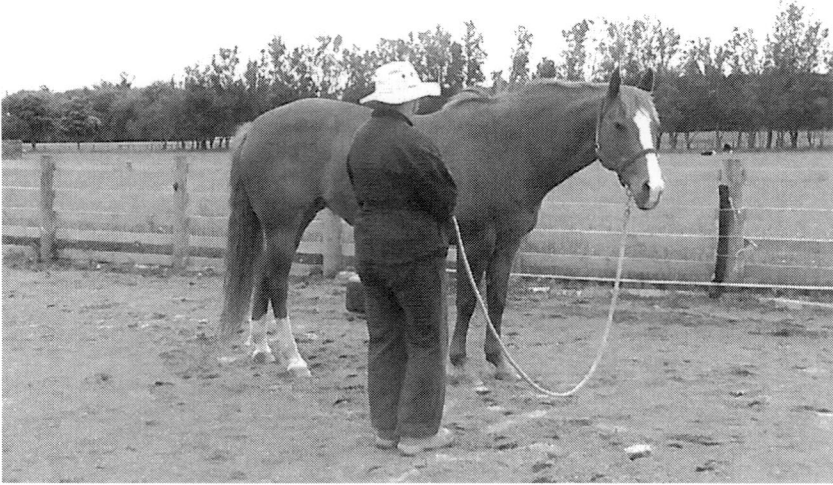

Figure 54: Pause between the notes. Relaxed postures.

14. As 13 above plus back up straight when I gently jiggle the rope from waist level as a signal *without moving my feet*? Relax (click&treat), pause. (See Figure 55.)

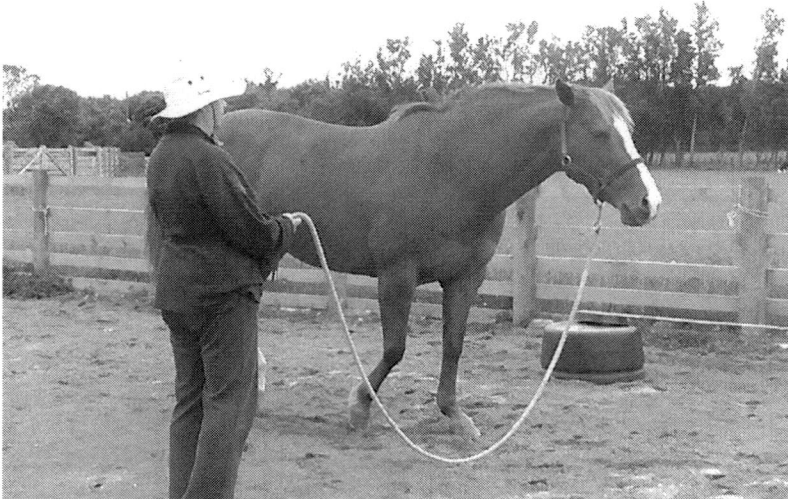

Figure 55: Sending a text message up the rope to signal, "Please step back".

33-10: Training Plan 6: One Step at a Time

Aim:

The horse willingly steps backwards and forward on request and can smoothly shift his balance from forward to halt to back-up to halt to forward. The halts are almost momentary.

Environment:
- Work in a space familiar to the horse, where he is usually relaxed.
- Have a halter and lead rope on the horse. A short lead rope (8') is best for this activity.
- Ensure he is in a learning frame of mind. If not, encourage activity to use up adrenalin or relax and play with things he knows to overcome anxiety, before starting.

This task is based on a passage in Dorrance (2001 edition), pages 125-128.

The skill of being able to ask your horse to move one specific foot at a time is a huge stepping stone. It is the beginning of a skill that will be used and refined when riding or doing ground work, including Horse Agility competition. It starts with being able to *visualize* the pattern in which horses move their feet.

Carefully observe how horses move their legs at walk, back-up, trot and canter. Reviewing slow motion video is best. Learn the footfall (foot-rise) for walk and trot, one gait at a time. When they are clear in your mind, add the canter.

Get down on all fours so you can mimic the pattern with your limbs. That helps put it into your deep memory. Once you can easily replay the memory tape for each gait in your mind, you can give your horse much clearer signals.

Time spent perfecting this helps to build the feel you will need when you want to time your riding or leading signals to the horse's feet.

This is a great task for teaching us to feel the horse's intent and to reward the slightest try by taking pressure off (click&treat). The ability to see and feel footfall (foot-rise) is what sets able horsemen apart from all the others.

Directing our horse's feet one at a time has many uses.

- Cleaning/trimming feet
- Positioning for mounting
- Backing into stalls/wash bays
- Breed and showmanship classes
- Leading through narrow spaces
- Trailer loading
- Precision riding
- Placing a foot for an x-ray
- Building communication/trust
- Mat work
- Pedestals
- Bridges
- Water obstacles
- Horse Agility obstacles.

Slices of the Process:

One Step Back

Much of the technique is illustrated in *#27 HorseGym with Boots.*

Visualize what you want. [*When I put light backward signal pressure on the halter, I want the horse to step back and relax/wait before moving another step back with the other foot and relax/wait, and so on*]. Think through your signal.

In order to lift his **right front** foot the horse has to shift his weight to his left shoulder and slightly back.

1. Face the horse, slightly to the side of his head and orientate your belly button toward his nose (when his head is straight).

2. Start by holding the rope about an arm's length from the halter, lightly draped.
3. Hold the rope in the hand nearest the horse's shoulder (*rope hand*).
4. Reach across with the other hand (*sliding* hand) and slide it smoothly up the rope toward the halter.
5. At some stage, you will reach a *point of contact* to which the horse will respond.
6. When you reach the *point of contact* tilt his nose/neck slightly to the left and put a bit of backward pressure on the halter. *Release immediately* when you feel his *intent* to move back (click&treat). Relax, then ask again.
7. When you get a whole step, release (click&treat), relax. Maybe rub him if you are not using Clicker Training. If you get more than one step, accept it, reward it, and then adjust your signal so it has less energy.

Some horses may at first respond by leaning into the backward pressure you are putting on the halter. They are not wrong because to move into pressure is a natural horse response. They are also not wrong because they don't yet understand what you want.

If your horse leans into the pressure:

1. Take up a power position (feet shoulder-width apart, one slightly ahead, hips dropped).
2. Hold the rope in the hand nearest the horse, about 2'-3' from the halter with a bit of slack in it.
3. Reach across with your other hand and softly run it up the rope toward the halter until you meet resistance from the horse.
4. At that point, simply 'hold' just strongly enough to make the horse feel unbalanced.
5. The moment he shows the slightest tendency to shift backwards to regain his balance, release the pressure (click&treat).

6. Repeat. If you are clear and consistent and release (click&treat) promptly, the horse will soon read your body language, energy, intent, and will step back before you can even slide your fingers up the rope.

When you reach the response in number 6 above you have created a gesture signal that you can also use at liberty to ask the horse to step back. Keep the gesture exactly as it was, i.e. running your hand up an imaginary rope.

When we have one step back at a light signal, we ask for two. It's important to 'release' the halter pressure slightly after the first step, the increase the pressure slightly to ask again for the second step before a bigger release (click&treat).

Once that is smooth, ask for three steps, then four, and so on until you have as many steps as you like. The horse will soon be able to read the intent in your body language and will keep stepping back until you turn off your 'intent'.

To move his *left front* foot back, tilt his nose/neck slightly to the right, i.e. *always tilt the nose away from the foot you want him to move.*

If the horse tends to push forward into the handler, it can help to stand the horse in a corner, or in a blocked-off lane, so that stepping back is the only easy and common sense thing to do.

When backing from the halt feels easy, we can expand and generalize the task by walking along beside the horse, halting and smoothly pivoting into position to face the horse and ask him to back up.

One Step Forward

Visualize what you want. [*When I put light forward signal pressure on the halter, I want the horse to step forward and relax/wait before moving another step forward with the other foot and relax/wait, and so on*]. Think through your signal.

To move one step forward, tilt his nose slightly away from the foot you want to move (to take the weight off it) and put forward pressure on the halter.

It took me a long time to get these moves firmly into my muscle memory. I had to learn to look carefully at where the horse's feet were already so I could decide which way I needed to tilt the head to move a particular foot. I'm not good with left/right or 3-dimensional thinking.

Eventually, get him to put a front foot on things. Start with a largish item like a doormat or a piece of carpet. Work toward smaller things like paper plates, Frisbees and leaves, then higher things like stumps, steps, pedestals, ramps, hoof stands.

Clicker Training works nicely for this.

Be aware that once the horse is close to the object he can't see it, but is working from memory. The area directly under his head/neck is a blind spot.

Be particular, but not critical. Always relax, pause and *re-set* if the horse seems worried. After a good effort, go away from that site and do other things the horse already knows.

Then come back to moving one foot until you get another good effort. Don't drill. After you've had two or three good attempts, stop and come back to it another time.

The essence of these moves is that you build signals that communicate to the horse about moving individual feet.

Reminder: three minutes of focused work over many sessions will get you there without lapsing into human or horse frustration.

In the end, every signal we give our horse is designed to get him to move his feet where we want them. Doing this task well helps you gain access to the horse's mind and through his mind you can organize his feet.

When we have one step forward at a light signal, we ask for two, then three, then four, and so on until we have as many steps as we like.

Do a few each session until you are both good at it. Refresh it often.

Generalization

Be sure to teach 'one step at a time' standing on the horse's left side and on his right side. If he finds one side harder, work at bit more on that side.

Most people will find the side where they use their less dominant hand harder as well. When each side feels the same, you've reached a big milestone.

When we can use a light signal to ask the horse to glide from walk into a halt and straight into a smooth back-up, we have achieved our task.

33-11: Training Plan 7: Head Down & Head Up

Aim:

The horse willingly lowers and raises his head, on request.

Environment:
- Work in a space familiar to the horse, where he is usually relaxed.
- Ensure he is in a learning frame of mind. If not, encourage activity to use up adrenalin or relax and play with things he knows to overcome anxiety, before starting.

If we can ask a horse to drop his head, in certain situations it allows us to help him lower his adrenalin and anxiety levels.

But it needs to be used judiciously, since a highly-adrenalized horse (fearful or excited) is often better off if we do something that allows him to work the adrenalin off through active movement.

If a horse is moderately anxious, head lowering is a way we can teach him to calm himself down, so it is worth teaching.

We counter-balance 'Head Down' with 'Head Up' techniques.

A: 'Head Down' with Rope Signal

1. Have a halter and a lead rope on your horse.
2. Visualize what you want. [*I want his head to drop down when I put light downward pressure on the lead rope and I want his head to come up with light upward pressure on the halter.*] Think your signal.
3. Bend, sit, or kneel so you can comb (milk) the lead rope toward the ground to put downward pressure on the halter. Release (click&treat) the instant he drops his head even the tiniest bit, *or even just stops bracing upwards against the pressure.* As soon as you feel either of these, open your hand fully to stop all pressure (click&treat), relax, let him put his head up again if he wants. You are not trying to hold his head down.
4. If he doesn't lower his head with combing/milking the rope, tighten your fingers on the rope one at a time, watching carefully for the slightest try — even a tiny movement or thought downwards, and immediately open your hand (click&treat). Relax. Wait. Start again. You are re-setting the task. There is no right and wrong because the horse does not yet understand what you are asking.
5. Your aim is to have the head come down with very light signal pressure on the rope, so always start with light combing of the rope. If the horse is still unsure, tighten the fingers as you comb the rope.
6. If he is still unsure, hold the rope at an even tightness, letting your hand go up with him if he pulls his head up (opposition reflex). Keep the tension as steady as you can, until he figures out that dropping his head (release /click&treat) is the only way to get rid of the pressure.
7. Once he understands the game, it pays to do it regularly to keep it fresh in his repertoire.

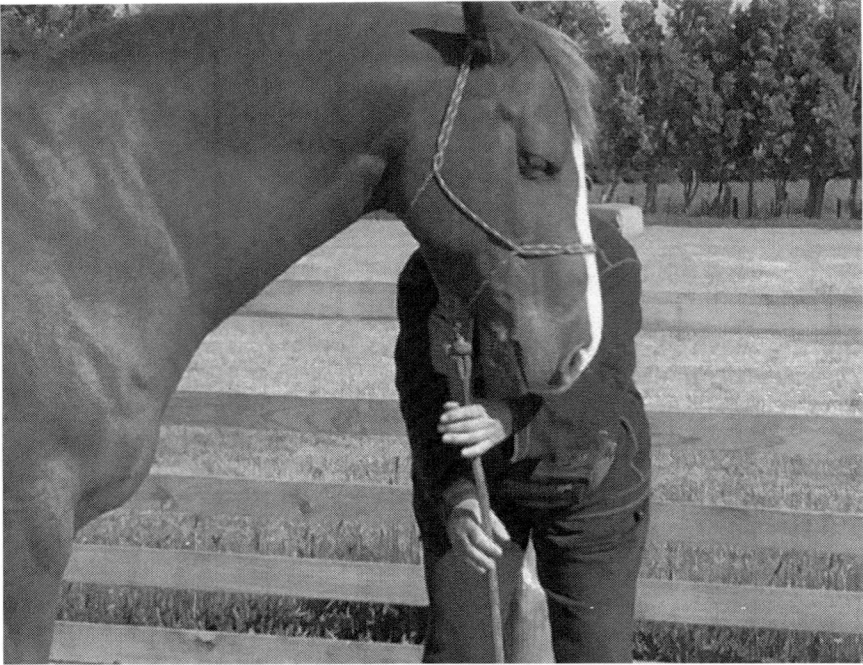

Figure 56: I'm gently 'milking' ('combing') the lead rope with my fingers to ask for 'head down please'.

Asking for 'Head Up'

To bring his head up, hold the rope straight up past his ears and jiggle it gently. Stop jiggling (click&treat) as soon as it begins to come up.

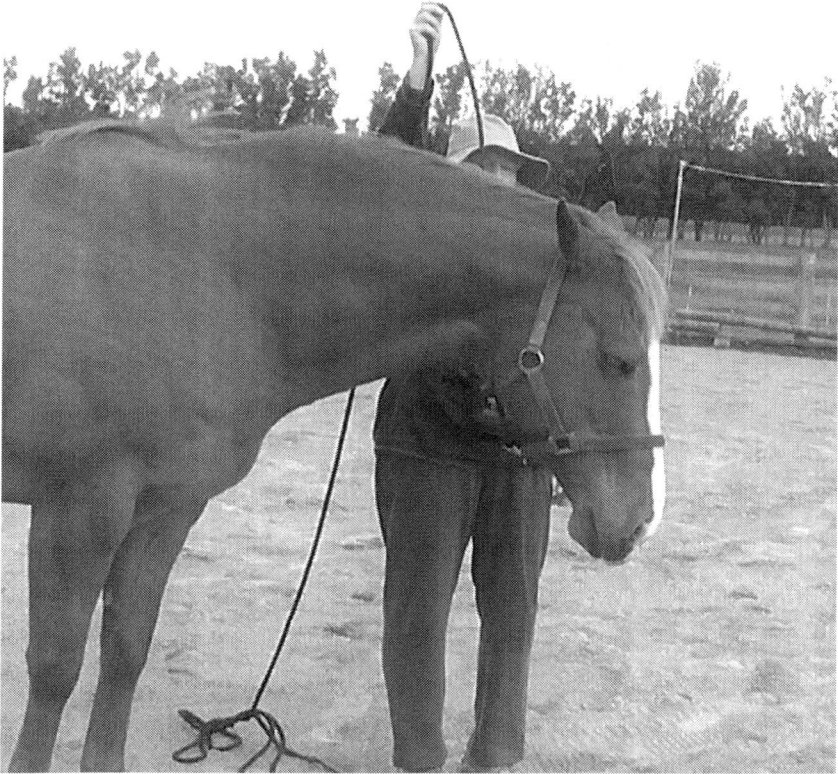

Figure 57: For 'head up please', gently jiggle the rope straight upwards.

B: 'Head Down' with Poll Signal

1. Do this once your horse is confident about you rubbing his head and neck.
2. Visualize what you want. [*When I put pressure on his poll I want him to drop his head*]. Rub his poll. Think through your signal.
3. Keep his head straight by holding the rope, near the halter, with your other hand.

4. Standing beside your horse, gently press on his poll with your thumb and forefinger. Increase the pressure gradually until he moves his head down away from the pressure (click&treat). <u>Don't follow his head down</u>. Immediately when he moves his head down even a tiny bit, or even just stops bracing upwards against your fingers, run your hand down his neck to his withers in a friendly way (click&treat). Relax.
5. Then start again, rub his poll, gently press, and so on.

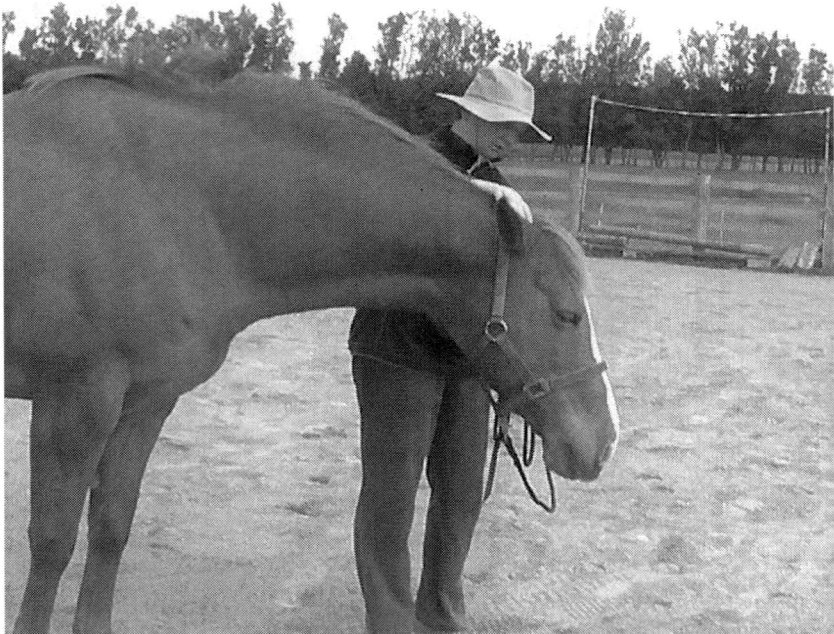

Figure 58: To ask for 'head down please', apply gentle signal pressure at the poll.

Asking for 'Head Up'

To bring his head up, put an index finger from each hand into the jugular groove on each side of his head and press gently, releasing (click&treat) the instant the head moves up. Be sure to keep your head well to the side, not hovering over his neck.

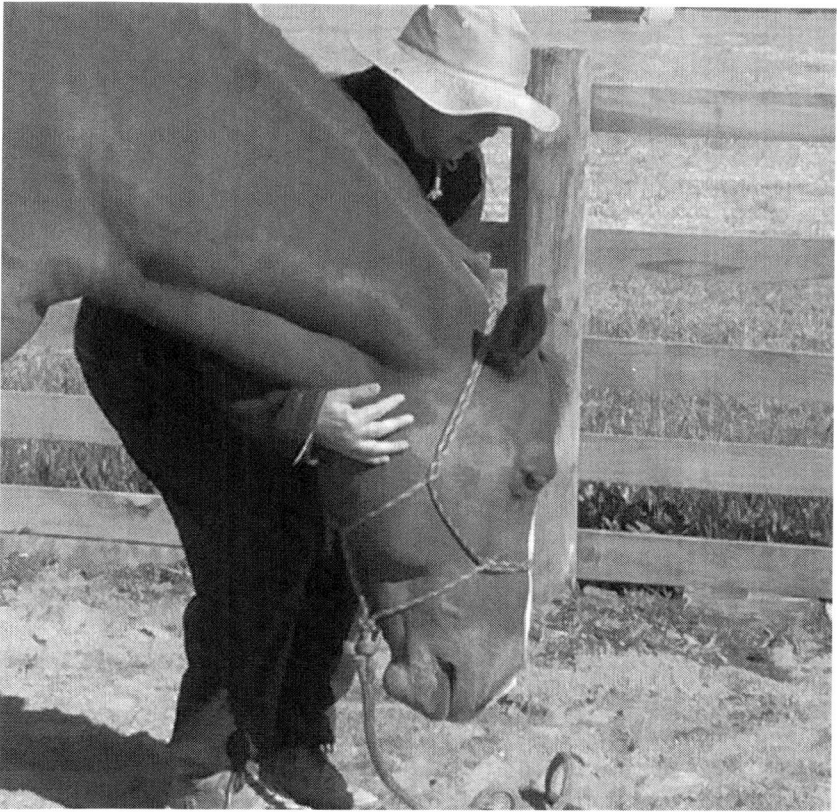

Figure 59: Gentle finger pressure in the jugular groove each side of the neck can be used as a signal for 'head up please'. Be sure to keep your head well to one side in case the horse pops his head up suddenly.

C: Head Down with Targeting

If we have taught the horse to become clicker savvy by touching his nose to an object in our hand to earn a click&treat, we can ask him to lower his head by gradually holding the object closer and closer to the ground.

Detailed information about Clicker Training can be found in my book, *How to Begin Equine Clicker Training*.

Once the horse has the idea, we can focus on balance and skeletal alignment by carefully locating the target object to keep the horse straight through his body. We can also adjust the placement of the target to cause him to flex slightly to the left or the right.

For 'head up', move the target object up again. Once the horse understands the 'head down' and 'head up' movements by following the target, we can add verbal, gesture or touch signals.

D: Head Down with Modelling

We can teach a clicker savvy horse to drop his head using a behavior capturing process called *free-shaping*. We capture a specific behavior by watching for it to occur naturally and marking it with a click&treat.

Instead of putting signal pressure on the horse, we observe in a relaxed manner until the horse lowers his head even a tiny bit: click&treat.

Because the horse is motivated to find out what will result in a click&treat, it usually doesn't take long for him to work out that the 'click point' or 'desired behavior of the moment' is a lowering of his head.

By gradually withholding the click until the head drops a bit further, we can get it all the way down to the ground as well as have it stay down a bit longer.

Once the horse freely offers the behavior, we can add a signal. It's also good to add a verbal or gesture signal for 'head up'.

The process is illustrated in my *Free-Shaping Examples* playlist in the two clips called *Head-lowering*.

33-12: Training Plan 8: Light rope/rein Response

This Training Plan builds nicely onto Training Plan 5: *Rope Texting* (Part 33-9).

Light rein response means that the horse responds willingly, without brace, when we signal him to either drop his nose vertically and/or flex right or left at the poll vertebrae so we can direct his nose. The key to both of these is to have clear, consistent signals which have been carefully taught.

All resistance in the horse's head and body begins in the horse's mind. If a horse is resistant to rope or rein pressure, there will be a reason.

Either he has not been carefully taught with clear, consistent signals, or he has experienced discomfort, pain or mouth trauma in the past.

If it is discomfort, pain or trauma, these are triggered in his mind, resulting in immediate mental and emotional anxiety and resistance as soon as the tools appear.

Either way, to improve pulling on the reins or evasion of rope/rein signals, whether we are leading, riding or long-reining, it is easier for the horse if we begin on the ground. It allows us to work through all the stages and find the sticky places.

Once we have a feel for where the horse becomes uncomfortable, we can develop an Individual Education Program (IEP) that builds on the horse's current understanding. To achieve a light rein response, the horse needs total confidence in our hands.

The IEP you write could take a week, a month, or several months to achieve. The goal is to establish or re-establish a horse's mental and emotional trust in a particular person's hands. The way many horses are introduced to halter and bit pressure gives them little reason to trust people's hands on a rope or a set of reins.

A horse with minimal negative experience will most likely be a dream to teach. A horse with a history of unsympathetic handling around his head will probably take much longer.

The thin slices that follow are all done standing beside the horse behind his withers, where we would be if riding. Standing on a safe platform gives us the reach to activate both right and left reins.

All the slices are carried out from both the left and right sides. Often it makes sense to teach one slice on the left, then the same slice on the right. But this is not a rule. Sometimes we may decide to teach several slices on one side before beginning again on the other side.

Depending on how ambidextrous the horse is in his muscles and his mind, he may find one side much harder than the other. Likewise, humans usually have a dominant side and their signals will be clearer when using their dominant side.

Both horse and person will experience more natural resistance when using the less dominant side of their body because the nerve pathways to activate those muscles are not strongly built and the muscles themselves are less toned.

The most interesting challenges arise when both the horse and the handler are striving to use their less dominant side at the same time.

Being aware that this is a normal challenge encourages us to spend the time and effort needed to get both sides evened out, allowing both the horse and the hander to improve ease of communication and ease of movement without the interruption of emotional turmoil or confusion.

It doesn't take much lateral flexion of the head to ask for change of direction when riding or long-reining. We don't need to ask for lots of bend as we teach this. The aim is to have the horse release the poll vertebrae easily at our signal. We are not trying to pull the whole neck around.

Yielding of the poll vertebrae is what delivers a 'soft yield of the nose' or a 'softening of the jaw' which, to me, has always been a strange expression because a horse can't actually 'give' with his jaw unless he opens his mouth or we are thinking of his whole cheekbone as his jaw.

The softening is first in his mind (no resistance to the signal) and then in his poll so we can lightly direct his nose right or left. Once he agrees in his mind and gives us the flexion, his weight will shift and his feet will follow our suggestion.

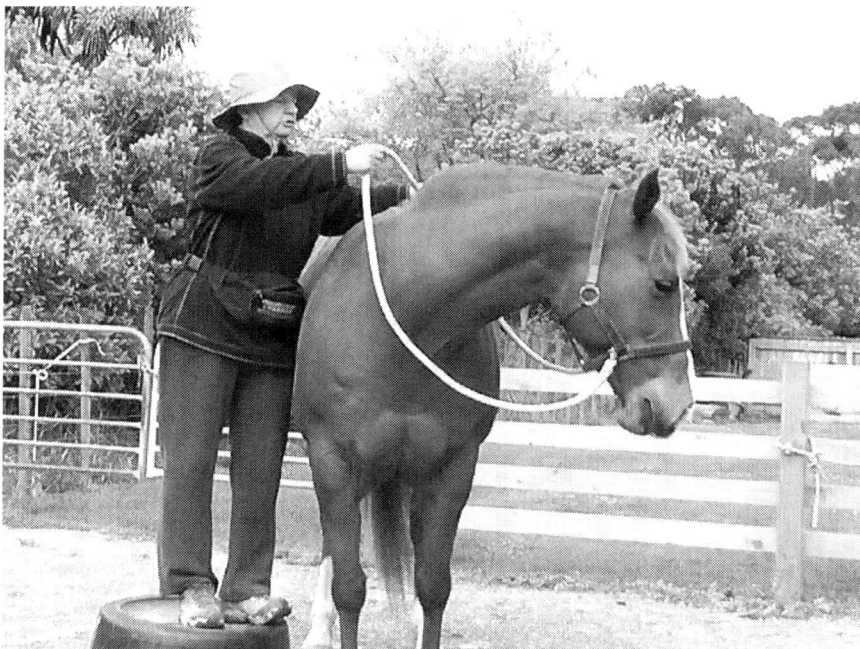

Figure 60: Standing behind the withers to teach soft yield to the rein. Note, to use the far rein I need to begin by lifting the rein with my outside hand so I can use the hand closest to the horse to run softly up the rope toward the halter to a 'point of contact' to which the horse responds.

Aim:

When we put light pressure on the rein or rope from a position standing beside the horse's ribs, we would like the horse to give at the poll so his nose moves in the direction of our signal (follows the feel).

This work is illustrated in five short clips found in my YouTube playlist called *Developing Soft Rein Response*.

Environment:

- To start, it helps enormously if the horse is standing in a safe corner or at least alongside a safe fence. 'Safe' means barriers through which the horse can't put his feet if he suddenly moves back or sideways. Safe corners can be created with barrels or jump stands and rails.
- If you think the horse might take the signal to mean 'back up', stand him with his butt against a safe barrier (non-wire fence/gate, hedge, line of barrels, stall wall)
- Have the horse in a familiar, comfortable environment.
- If the horse is already mat savvy, we can park his front feet on a mat.
- Horse is wearing a halter and lead. A shorter rope is probably better for this exercise.
- You also need a set of reins that attach to the side of the halter for Slice Three onwards.
- Unless the horse is a pony shorter than the handler's shoulders, we need a safe platform (mounting block) that allows us to reach across the withers to activate the rein on the far side.
- Handler position is beside the horse's ribs, just behind the withers, facing forward.
- Ensure the horse is in a relaxed, learning frame of mind. If not, encourage activity to use up adrenalin or relax and play with things he knows, to overcome anxiety before starting.
- Very short (3-minute) lessons over many days usually give the best result.
- The release/click point for all this work is any willing 'release' of the nose/jaw (via the poll) into our hand's light signal pressure.

- When the horse can't yet offer the flexion we want, rather than increase the signal pressure, it is best to *pretend* the horse did it, release and relax (but not click&treat if using Clicker Training) then *re-set the task* and ask again. This seems to work because it stops frustration building up in the handler. To the horse, it is probably a fairly neutral action, because he has no idea what we want at this point. Eventually you will get a soft response to a soft signal, at which point it is time to celebrate hugely.

For slices *One* to *Nine*, we want the horse standing still and relaxed, i.e. remaining 'parked'.

Slice One: Yield to Gentle Rhythmic Rope Pressure

1. Handler (on the ground for this part) moves to stand beside the horse's ribs just behind the withers, facing forward, rope in the hand closest to the horse. Asks *horse to remain facing forward*: relaxed body language (click&treat).
2. Gently use both hands to 'milk' the rope, putting light pressure on the halter, looking for the slightest 'give' of the horse's nose toward you. Release (click&treat). Walk to stand in front of the horse to re-set his head straight forward. If using Clicker Training, deliver the treat from in front for the same reason.
3. Repeat 1 and 2 until the horse waits for the touch signal on the halter and willingly yields his nose.
4. If he begins to turn his head as soon as you move back into position behind his withers, wait until he straightens his head: relax, turn away a bit, and maybe change position to stand in front of him again. (click&treat – moving in front of him to deliver the treat).
5. As mentioned before, this could all happen very quickly or it could take multiple short sessions.

Slice Two: Yield to Smooth Rope Signal

6. When the response to your 'milking the rope' signal is tidy on both sides, change to lifting the rope with the hand nearest the horse. Reach across and run the fingers of your outside hand gently up the rope toward the halter: release (click&treat) at the smallest indication of the nose yielding toward you.

7. Be sure to teach this on both sides. It may be considerably harder for the horse on one side. Avoid the trap of expecting the horse to understand because you've just spent ages teaching it on the other side.

8. When you feel ready, take the horse away from the barrier on the far side and see if you still have a nice tidy response. If using a mat, also check if it works cleanly without a mat. If things are not smooth at the first attempt without the support of barrier or mat, go back to them right away before the horse has a chance to experiment with evasive habits that will cloud his correct response.

9. We need each slice of the overall task to be clean and tidy before asking more.

Slice Three: Introduce Reins and Platform

10. When slice 2 is good, exchange the lead rope for a set of reins attached to the side rings of a halter. If the reins have no central buckle, wrap tape where a buckle would be so you can easily see and feel where the middle of the rein is. Ask the horse to stand beside your platform or mounting block, putting your torso above his withers. With a small pony, you won't need the platform.

11. Make sure the horse is comfortable standing beside the platform and with you getting on and off the platform. If he is not comfortable, add teaching this to your Individual Education Program and work on it first.

12. Put the reins over the horse's head. Stand on the platform facing forward, shoulder-to-shoulder with the horse. Rest the hand closest to the horse on the 'buckle' (tape) of the rein. The goal is to be able to do this and *the horse stays relaxed, facing forward.* If he can do so for one second, release the rein, (click&treat), step off platform, relax.
13. It's fine if the horse flexes his poll vertically when he feels your hand on the rein. When the horse gets 10/10 standing relaxed, head forward after you step onto the platform and rest your hand on the rein, it is time for the next slice.

Slice Four: Lift Rein

14. Slice Four repeats slice Three, but this time, as well as putting your hand on the 'buckle' of the rein, also lift the rein an inch or two, as you would when riding from a halt into a walk. You are starting to activate the rein.
15. When the horse fully understands that your hand on the rein or lifting the rein is *not* a signal for him to flex left or right, you can begin to ask for flexion toward the side you are standing on.

Slice Five: Yield Nose toward Handler

16. After lifting the rein (about six inches above the withers) in the hand nearest the horse, run your other hand gently up the rein toward the halter. Watch for the slightest tendency to bring the nose toward you: release (click) step to the front of the horse to deliver the treat or stand in relaxed mode if not using Clicker Training. Stepping to the front of the horse will bring his nose straight again.

17. This can be complicated for the horse because we are teaching two 'opposite' moves. We want 'head straight' while we get into position and put a hand on the rein. Then we want 'yield the nose' when we give the halter touch signal via the rein. It is much easier for the horse to distinguish these two moves if we use Clicker Training. If we are using release reinforcement, we only have relaxation of our body energy and a kind word (maybe a rub if the horse likes being touched) to let the horse know when he is 'right' in our eyes.

18. If the horse offers the yield as soon as you step onto the platform, simply wait until he puts his head forward again: praise, rub, (click&treat) before giving the rein signal.

19. If he yields as soon as you touch the rein, that is okay for now. When you start asking for yield to the other side, he will learn to wait to feel which side you are requesting.

20. Start by releasing for even a hint of response to the signal.

21. As the horse's understanding develops, ask for a bit more before the release (click&treat). We don't need a huge bend. We just want a willing release of the nose/jaw, via the poll, in response to our hand's light signal pressure.

22. When the horse is comfortable yielding toward the handler, we can change the parameter to asking for a yield away from the side the handler is on.

Slice Six: Putting our Outside Hand on the Rein for nose yielding away

23. When we ask the horse to bend the other way, he may think that we want him to back up. It is helpful to have a safe barrier behind him.

24. Pick up the 'buckle' of the rein with the hand *furthest* from the horse. (See figure 60.) This causes a shift in your body orientation. The horse notices this shift and it will become part of the signal package for asking him to bend away from the side you are on.

Slice Seven: Yield Nose Away from the Handler

25. As for Slice Four, we want the horse to be comfortable with our new body position, i.e., lifting the rein one or two inches with our outside hand. We want him to keep his head straight.

26. As before, if the horse offers the yield as soon as you step onto the platform, simply wait until he puts his head forward again: praise, rub, (click&treat) before giving the rein signal.

27. To ask for the yield away, lift the rein about six inches above the withers with the hand furthest from the horse (while facing forward) and gently slide your rein hand toward the halter on the far side of the withers (see Figure 60).

28. Release (click&treat) at the smallest suggestion of the nose moving away from you. If you watched my relevant video clips, they give an excellent example of how to confuse a horse by not releasing (click&treating) promptly when the horse is in the 'acquisition' stage of a new skill.

29. If the horse seems confused, use your fingers to stroke the rope rather than put steady pressure on it. A horse easily braces against steady pressure, but a rhythmic feel on the rein will encourage him to think through the request. Stop and celebrate after one or two successful responses. He will think on that and it will be easier next time.

30. These teaching/learning sessions should stay very short. We can go away to do other things between short 'soft rein response' sessions or wait until the next day.

Slice Eight: Mixing up Right and Left

31. When we have reliable responses for all of the above from both sides of the horse, we can begin to mix up asking for flexion toward the handler or away from the handler.

32. It may seem simple to us, but it requires the horse to understand each part (head straight, head toward handler, head away from handler) and not 'jump the gun' to offer what he thinks we are going to ask.

33. It pays to pause between each request. I like to add a 'head straight' verbal signal, which I also use later for long-reining. We can also add the left and right verbal signals we'll use with long-reining. Before adding a verbal signal, the horse should be offering the behavior reliably. Otherwise the verbal signal is meaningless.

34. If we mix up 'toward handler' and 'away from handler' randomly, the horse usually learns to wait for the direction signal.

35. If he flexes pro-actively, we just need to appreciate his keenness and spend more time relaxing him with his head straight.

Slice Nine: Adding a Bit

36. If we want to use a bit, we repeat the whole process from Slice Three onwards. If the horse has experienced discomfort, pain or trauma with a bit, this probably happened when the rider was aboard. The very fact of a rider on the horse's back will probably trigger 'bit' anxiety or resistance in his mind. It can take a lot of care and patience to over-come this sort of thing.

37. Often horses who strongly resist bits due to past pain and mouth trauma adapt with great relief to bit-less head gear.

Slice Ten: Long-Reining

38. If intending to long-rein, we can set up objects in a straight row and refine the rein signals from behind as we weave right and left between the objects. We have them far apart to start with, then gradually reduce the distance between them. I have always long-reined with a halter or side-pull headstall, rather than using a bit.

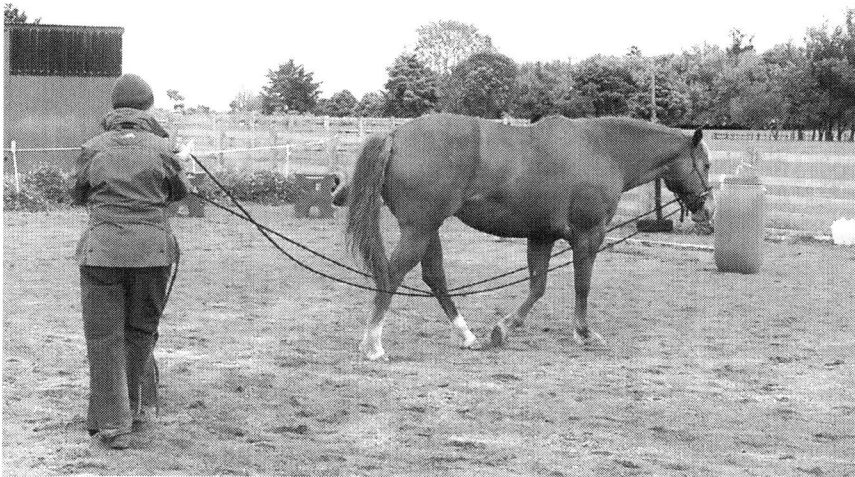

Figure 61: Long-reining is superb to teach the horse confidence with guidance from behind. It can also teach us to refine our direction signals to make them as light as possible. The horse feels everything. Note Bridget's open hand on the rein as she sends the signal to turn right.

39. The challenge will be to handle our reins with great finesse, allowing the horse to keep the soft response we have taught. The horse can only be as soft as our hands are soft.

40. A most interesting experience is to put the halter around our neck, hold the nosepiece in front of us with both hands, and have someone long-rein us from behind. (See figure 20.) Being 'the horse' for a variety of people made me understand why some horses don't want anything to do with people.

41. To begin with, we can use a boundary fence on one side and have mat or barrel destinations (rest or click&treat spots) at each end of the line of weave obstacles.
42. Then we can set up courses with obstacles to long-rein over, across, around, through, between, into and out of. We can set up 'gates' through which to navigate, driving a variety of patterns among the gates.

Slice Eleven: Riding

43. If we intend to ride, we start again, at the halt, with Slice Three. Here also, we can begin by using a safe barrier on one side, in front, or behind to avoid the choices of moving forward, backing up or swinging the hind end away. The idea is always to make what we want the easiest option.
44. When the rein responses are smooth and soft at the halt, we can walk weave patterns and gradually work up to large figure 8 patterns, 90 degree turns, 180 degree turns, 360 degree turns, arcs, curves and circles.
45. When all is smooth at the walk, we can incorporate trot and eventually canter.

Fashions, Traditions and Keeping an Open Mind

As we troll through the information available about how to keep and train horses, it seems that some of it is based on age-old tradition, much of it from the time when horses were the vehicles of war or the vehicles of boy-racers before the motor car came along.

Some of it is based on newer fashions such as Natural Horsemanship or a modern-day version of Vaquero style riding. Much of it revolves around using a horse as a tool for competition to bolster the human ego.

Horses are not easy to work with in a laboratory situation. Therefore, they have never had the attention given to rats and pigeons in terms of their learning styles and learning abilities. Scientific learning theory has been slow to trickle down to the world of horse owners.

Neither are horses special enough to pull large crowds as do the trained water mammals in places like Sea World, although Cavalia is now commercializing on the appeal that horses have for many people.

While clicker training for dogs has had some success, clicker training for horses is still seen by many as bizarre.

Sadly, some equine clicker trainers have become 'exclusive' which can be off-putting for people who would like to use it without having to negate everything else they are doing.

Here is an example to explain what I mean by 'fashion'.

To teach side-passing while riding, one trainer opens his leg on the side he wants the horse to move into and simultaneously puts his weight a bit more into the outside stirrup. To regain comfort, the horse learns to move away from the outside pressure toward the open leg.

To teach the same thing, another trainer shifts his weight to the side he wants the horse to move into. The horse learns to regain balance by shifting sideways so he is back underneath the rider.

As long as the rider is clear and consistent, the horse soon learns to respond to the consistent signal to regain comfort.

In other words, if we teach with.....
- clear precise signals used as lightly as possible
- thoughtful body language
- consistency
- awareness of what the horse is telling us
- an Individual Education Program based on each horse's character type, age, health, past experiences and ability to absorb new information

..... then we are doing the best we can.

Whether we use release reinforcement or a combination of release and reward, the horse appreciates, above all, clear and consistent communication.

Hopefully the ideas in this book will aid communication between horses and their people.

If you enjoyed this book, please write a review and share your thoughts with other readers.

If you'd like to contact me with observations or questions, you can reach me at my email: hertha.james@xtra.co.nz.

Acknowledgements

This book is dedicated to Lois Shaw of Vancouver Island, Canada who looked at my first notes about 'Signals' and suggested that they should become a book.

It is also dedicated to Lorraine Erith who showed me how any horse can understand us when we use natural horse body language.

I'd especially like to thank Bridget Evans for her on-going support as my sounding board, model and videographer.

Finally, this book would not read nearly as smoothly without the input of Larry Metcalf, of Missouri, USA, who ponders the position of each comma in my work, and queries my occasional flights of fancy or garbled sentences.

List of YouTube Video Clips

Most of the video clips are shorter than five minutes, so they are quick to watch and easy to review if you are interested in specific tasks.

To reach my channel, put *Hertha MuddyHorse* into the YouTube search engine. The Clips are in one of three playlists.

1. Most of the clips are in my *HorseGym with Boots* playlist. Each title is written as #_ *HorseGym with Boots*. For example, if you want to quickly find Clip number 22, simply put: *#22 HorseGym with Boots* into the YouTube search engine and it should come right up.
2. Some clips are in the *Free-Shaping Examples* playlist. These are named only, so to find a particular clip, go to that playlist and scroll down for the clip's name.
3. Other clips are in the *Thin-Slicing Examples* playlist. These are also only named, so you search the playlist for the title you want.

A list of all the current *HorseGym with Boots* Clips follows, as well as titles in the *Free-Shaping* and *Thin-Slicing* examples.

HorseGym with Boots Series

Topics are added to this series as they are created.

1. Introduction
2. Giving meaning to the click
3. Stationary nose targets
4. Parking at a nose target (also spooky new things to touch)
5. Putting behavior 'on cue'

6. Foot targets (also, free-shaping new behavior)
7. Backing up from the mat
8. Duration on the mat
9. Putting the mat target 'on cue'
10. Generalizing mats
11. Mat-a-thons
12. Chaining tasks
13. Anthem is new to nose targets (Anthem is a young quarter-horse)
14. Anthem is new to foot targets
15. Parking at a distance
16. The 'triple treat'
17. 'Walk-on' and 'halt' multi-cues
18. Parking out of sight
19. Free-shaping
20. The 'art of standing still'
21. Walk away for confidence (with new things)
22. Rope relaxation
23. Hosing on the mat (recognizing 'click points')
24. Parking commotions
25. Parking with ball commotion
26. 8 Leading Positions overview
27. Good Backing = Good Leading
28. Leading Position Three (beside neck or shoulder)
29. Leading Position Three with a 'circle of markers'
30. Leading Position Three duration exercise
31. Natural and Educated body language signals
32. Sensitivity to Body language
33. Opportunity, Signals 1
34. Signals 2: Gestures
35. Signals 3: Touch
36. Signals 4: Verbal signals (also environmental signals, horse initiated signals and marker signals)
37. Signals 5: Intent
38. Signals 6: Body Orientation (of handler)
39. Train with a Lane 1
40. Train with a Lane 2
41. Leading Position Seven Clip 1 of 4, in front facing horse
42. Leading Position Seven Clip 2 of 4

70. Weave Prep 4, Only the horse weaves
71. Weave Prep 5, Curves, Circles, at Liberty
72. Ground-tie Clip 1, Getting Started
73. Ground-tie Clip 2, Another Venue
74. Thin-slicing a Trailer Simulation
75. Quiet Sharing of Time and Place
76. Active Sharing of Time and Place + Greet & Go
77. Claim the Spot
78. Watchfulness First Action
79. Watchfulness Second & Third Actions
80. Guiding from Behind
81. Shadow Me
82. Boomerang Frolic
83. Shadow Me Duration with Clicker Training
84. Shadow Me Using Targets

Thin-Slicing Examples

This playlist includes thin-slicing examples about the following topics. To find a specific clip, go to the *Thin-Slicing Examples* playlist in my channel and scroll down to find the one you want. New clips are added as they are made.

- Tunnel with Boots
- Pool Noodle task
- Head Rocking for Poll Relaxation
- Bottle Bank obstacle
- Zigzag for Horse Agility
- Yield Shoulder into a Turn on the Haunches
- Stepping over rails
- Soft yield to Rein Signals (5 clips, also their own playlist)
- Thin-slice 'The Box' Movement (back, sideways, forward, sideways)
- Backing up
- Rope Texting
- Thin-slicing the 1m board
- Water & Tarp obstacle
- Thin-slice the 'Shadow Me' Game at Liberty
- Free-shape Learning to Ring a Bell

Free-Shaping Examples

This playlist includes clips using the free-shaping technique to teach a task. To find a particular clip, go to the *Free-Shaping Examples* playlist in my channel and scroll down to find the clip you want. Most of these clips show both free-shaping and thin-slicing.

- Table Manners for Clicker Training
- Boots and Bicycle
- Bob meets Bicycle (Bob is a young quarter horse)
- Introduction to a saddle (with Bob, his first meeting with a saddle)
- Head-lowering (2 Clips)
- Clicker 1 with Smoky
- Smoky and Dumb-bell target
- Boots picks up the Dumb-bell
- Free-shape Learning to Ring a Bell

There are also short playlists on specific topics including:

- Thin-slicing the Wagon-wheel obstacle
- Teaching the S-bend
- Soft Yield to Rein Signals (5 clips)
- Hula Hoop Challenges (5 clips)
- Single Obstacle Challenges
- 2012 Horse Agility
- 2014 Horse Agility
- 2015 Horse Agility
- 2016 Horse Agility

Most of the Horse Agility clips have a commentary explaining the tasks and showing where we lost marks. Each task is marked out of ten, five points for the handler and five points for the horse. Some are at liberty and others are with halter and lead. Horse Agility is at www.thehorseagilityclub.com.

Further Resources Available from the Author

Hard Copy Book:

Natural Horsemanship Study Guide

Available by contacting me at: hertha.james@xtra.co.nz.

Natural Horsemanship Study Guide. (2012). Powerword Publications; Palmerston North, NZ. The Book is in 2 volumes, over 400 pages, well-illustrated, indexed, referenced, supported with three DVDs.

This book brings together the philosophy and basic methodology of the worldwide movement called Natural Horsemanship. It looks in detail at ground work up to and including trailer loading, saddling and unsaddling.

The underlying aim of Natural Horsemanship is to teach us to work with the horse's nature rather than struggle against it.

The book is presented in two volumes so that it is easy to cross-reference the lesson plans in Volume 2 with the extensive information in Volume 1. It is a hands-on study guide complete with:

- a glossary with detailed notes covering key words and concepts
- a step-by-step guide to learning *International Horse Language*, all done at liberty
- outlines to help you get good at 'reading your horse'
- practical exercises toward smooth gear handling
- goal setting and easy recording of your progress
- guidelines to help create good lesson plans for any specific horse
- clear, detailed information showing you how to teach your horse nine basic ground moves, polite saddling, drive-by grooming and trailer-loading.
- sequential lesson plans including written tasks to speed up learning of concepts and terminology, as well as practical tasks to develop your skills.

DVD & Notes Sets:

Available by contacting me at hertha.james@xtra.co.nz.

Teaching Long-Reining with Positive Reinforcement

This DVD and 26-page booklet breaks long-reining into its smallest teachable parts. Then it shows Smoky going through the initial learning process and Boots demonstrating some of the finer points.

Harness Horse Prep using Positive Reinforcement

This DVD and 23-page booklet go through the stages of developing a horse's confidence to wear harness, hitch up and pull a cart at home in a controlled situation.

My Other Books Available from Amazon.com.

You can find these books any time by putting my name (Hertha James) into the Amazon search engine. A short review on Amazon is always appreciated.

- ***How to Begin Equine Clicker Training***: *Improve Horse-Human Communication*
- ***Walking with Horses***: *The Eight Leading Positions*
- ***Learn Universal Horse Language***: *No Ropes*
- ***How to Create Good Horse Training Plans***: *The Art of Thin-Slicing*

If you prefer e-books but don't have a Kindle reader, Amazon has a free Kindle reader which can be downloaded to any computer, tablet or smartphone.

Reference List

Abrantes, Roger.DVDs (2013). *The 20 Principles all Animal Trainers Must Know.* Tawzer Dog LLC. www.TawzerDog.com

Bruce, Georgia. (2013). *How to Teach Your Horse Tricks with Clicker Training.* Kuranda, Australia. www.ClickerTraining.org

Budiansky, Stephen. (1997). *The Nature of the Horse: Their Evolution, Intelligence and Behavior.* Phoenix; London.

Burns, Stephanie. (2002). *Move Closer Stay Longer.* Parelli Natural Horsemanship; Pagosa Springs, Colorado. (Excellent if you feel nervous around horses.)

Camp, Joe (2011). *Training with Treats: with relationship & basic training locked in, treats can become an excellent way to enhance good communication.* 14 Hands Press; USA.

Dorrance, Bill and Desmond, Leslie. (2001). *True Horsemanship Through Feel.* First Lyons Press; Guilford, CT.

Hanson, Mark. (2011). *Revealing Your Hidden Horse: a revolutionary approach to understanding your horse.* (Amazon On-Demand Publishing; www.amazon.com.)

Kurland, Alexandra. (www.theclickercenter.com)

MacLeay, Jennifer. (2003). *Smart Horse: understanding the science of natural horsemanship.* Blood Horse Publications; Lexington, Ky.

Miller, Dr Robert M. (1999). *Understanding the Ancient Secrets of the Horse's Mind.* The Russell Meerdink Co. Ltd.; Neenah, WI, USA. (Also, look up Dr Miller to find his resources on Foal Imprinting if you'd like to know more about that.)

Parelli, Pat and Linda Parelli. (www.parelli.com)

Pryor, Karen. (1999). *Don't Shoot the Dog: the new art of teaching and training.* Bantam; New York. (About much more than dogs.)

Pryor, Karen. (2009). *Reaching the Animal Mind: Clicker Training and what it teaches us about all animals.* Scribner; New York.

Pryor, Karen. (2014). *On My Mind: reflections on animal behavior and learning.* Sunshine Books Inc.; Waltham, MA, USA.

Resnick, Carolyn. (2005). *Naked Liberty: Memoirs of my Childhood: the language of movement, communication, and leadership through the way of horses.* Amigo Publications; Los Olivos, CA.

Schneider, Susan M. (2012). *The Science of Consequences: how they affect genes, change the brain and impact our world.* Prometheus Books; New York.

Printed in Great Britain
by Amazon